T0358628

Absolute Essentials of Marketing Research

This short textbook provides students with a concise yet comprehensive overview of the fundamentals of marketing research.

Mapped closely to the structure of a typical Marketing Research module, the book takes the student through the full process, from developing the hypothesis and setting the research question, to developing and conducting the research, and finally to analysing the data and making recommendations. Each chapter starts with an essential summary and ends with discussion questions that can be used as a teaching resource. Worksheets are also provided as a supplementary resource, which can be used to build a marketing research plan.

Focused on the core aspects of the subject, this is a perfect complement to the larger texts available, suitable for any undergraduate or postgraduate Marketing Research module.

Bonita M. Kolb is Professor Emeritus of Business Administration at Lycoming College, USA, and is currently researching the hospitality sector in St. Augustine, Florida.

Absolute Essentials of Business and Economics

Textbooks are an extraordinarily useful tool for students and teachers, as is demonstrated by their continued use in the classroom and online. Successful textbooks run into multiple editions, and in endeavouring to keep up with developments in the field, it can be difficult to avoid increasing length and complexity.

This series of Shortform textbooks offers a range of books which zero in on the absolute essentials. In focusing on only the core elements of each sub-discipline, the books provide a useful alternative or supplement to traditional textbooks.

Absolute Essentials of Business Behavioural Ethics
Nina Seppala

Absolute Essentials of Corporate Governance
Stephen Bloomfield

Absolute Essentials of Business Ethics
Peter A. Stanwick & Sarah D. Stanwick

Absolute Essentials of Creative Thinking and Problem Solving
Tony Proctor

Absolute Essentials of Environmental Economics
Barry C. Field

Absolute Essentials of Marketing Research
Bonita M. Kolb

For more information about this series, please visit: www.routledge.com/ Absolute-Essentials-of-Business-and-Economics/book-series/ABSOLUTE

Absolute Essentials of Marketing Research

Bonita M. Kolb

Routledge
Taylor & Francis Group

LONDON AND NEW YORK

First published 2022
by Routledge
2 Park Square, Milton Park, Abingdon, Oxon OX14 4RN

and by Routledge
605 Third Avenue, New York, NY 10158

Routledge is an imprint of the Taylor & Francis Group, an informa business

British Library Cataloguing-in-Publication Data
A catalogue record for this book is available from the British Library

Library of Congress Cataloging-in-Publication Data
Names: Kolb, Bonita M., author.
Title: Absolute essentials of marketing research / Bonita M. Kolb.
Description: Abingdon, Oxon ; New York, NY : Routledge, 2022. |
  Series: Absolute essentials of business and management | Includes
  bibliographical references and index.
Identifiers: LCCN 2021037092 (print) | LCCN 2021037093 (ebook) |
  ISBN 9780367760335 (hardback) | ISBN 9780367760342
  (paperback) | ISBN 9781003165194 (ebook)
Subjects: LCSH: Marketing research.
Classification: LCC HF5415.2 .K588 2022 (print) |
  LCC HF5415.2 (ebook) | DDC 658.8/3—dc23
LC record available at https://lccn.loc.gov/2021037092
LC ebook record available at https://lccn.loc.gov/2021037093

ISBN: 978-0-367-76033-5 (hbk)
ISBN: 978-0-367-76034-2 (pbk)
ISBN: 978-1-003-16519-4 (ebk)

DOI: 10.4324/9781003165194

Typeset in Times New Roman
by Apex CoVantage, LLC

Access the Support Material: www.routledge.com/9780367760335

Contents

Introduction

Marketing research plays a critical role in the creation of both an organization's strategic marketing plan and its overall strategic mission. This book is meant to be a user-friendly overview of the entire marketing research process. It covers quantitative, qualitative, and social media methods of conducting consumer research. These research tools can be used to uncover consumer preferences, experiences, and lifestyles. This information is needed when an organization is deciding what consumer segment to target and what product to introduce. It is also useful when deciding on the correct distribution, pricing, and promotion of a product. The critical issue of determining the right research question is covered, and the book also offers guidance on how to find the right research participants. The reader will find step-by-step instructions on how to use the research tools of surveys, focus groups, interviews, observation, and projective techniques. The book will then explain how to analyse the resulting data so that the organization will have strategic recommendations that can be implemented.

DOI: 10.4324/9781003165194-1

1 Understanding the research process

Type of research and the research profession

Research that is conducted can be divided into two types. Basic, or pure research, is used to discover new knowledge. When the research is planned and conducted, how the knowledge might be used to solve a problem is not of importance. What is important is that new information is discovered. After the research has been conducted, how the information can be used is then considered. Universities, governments, or very large corporations conduct most basic research.

Applied research that is used in marketing has a different purpose. The research is planned so that the findings can be used to solve a specific consumer or product problem. This is the type of research conducted by marketing professionals working either within an organization or for an external marketing research provider. After all, if a business is paying for research to be conducted, it needs results that will show how to solve a problem so that sales and revenue are increased. Most businesses do not have the time or money to pay for basic research.

Applied research should result in information that can be used to assist in making decisions. The decision might be critical and costly, such as which new product to introduce. Or the decision might be of lesser importance, such as what colours should be used on a website. The rationale of all applied marketing research is to help organizations limit the risk of making the wrong decision, because making mistakes about consumers or products can result in lost revenue.

Decisions that carry significant risk, such as new product introductions, will require a great deal of research. Such decisions may require a full-scale research project combining more than one research method. These types of studies may require the recruitment of a large number of research participants. Conducting the research will be costly, but the expense is acceptable because making a wrong decision will result in a very expensive mistake or even the end of the business. A small decision, such as what colours to use in on a website, still needs marketing research to eliminate risk, but the

DOI: 10.4324/9781003165194-2

research can be on a much smaller scale because the risk, which here is only the cost of redesigning the website, is less.

Research profession responsibilities

Job responsibilities within a marketing research firm or department at the lowest level will include tabulating results and assisting in preparing final reports. Positions with more authority would include professionals who plan research projects, analyse data, and write the reports. Specialized responsibilities would include people trained to conduct specific types of research, such as focus group moderators, and statisticians who are skilled in working and interrupting large volumes of data. Managing the effort would be the task of a research director who would report to the client who hired the research firm or, if the research department is in a large firm, to upper management. However, today all businesspeople and those working in non-profits should understand marketing research skills because they are critical to successfully managing any type of organization (Zimmerman 2018). Because non-profit organizations have other constituencies besides their customers or clients, they may also need to research beneficiaries of their services and the donors that support their work.

The field of marketing research is being changed by new technologies. The availability of online software tools and cell phone apps for both surveys and focus groups means that everyone working in marketing is now expected to have a basic understanding of the research process and the ability to conduct their own research. The ability to analyse and gain insights from consumer online comments is now an expected skill.

Research and the marketing plan

Research is too often thought of as only being useful in solving occasional marketing problems. It is true that research is needed to answer such questions as what types of new products consumers might want or what new market segments to target for an existing product. However, it is better to understand marketing research as a tool that should be used on a continual basis for finding new opportunities and solving problems.

Research also plays a critical role in the development of a comprehensive marketing plan for all types of businesses and organizations, both large and small and for-profit and non-profit. Marketing research is needed during the entire process of developing the marketing strategy. For example, the decision of which market segment to target cannot be chosen without researching the demographics of the consumer marketplace. Next, additional consumer research will be needed to determine what consumers in this target segment need and want. Finally, decisions about product, distribution, pricing, and promotion can only be successfully answered after conducting marketing research.

Steps in the research process

Too often, when a company conducts research, it begins without proper planning. However, the chances of finding the correct answer to a research question are greatly increased by following a specific six-step process. The process starts with determining what the organization needs to know and where it can find the information. In addition, researchers must determine who will participate in the research and the number of participants that will be needed. Researchers must then decide which research approach is appropriate for the research question and then choose the most suitable research method. The next step would be to plan the process of conducting the research. After the research is conducted, the final step will be to analyse and report the findings and recommendations.

Research process

1   Determine the research question.
2   Decide on sources of information and participants.
3   Choose the right approach.
4   Plan the research method.
5   Conduct the research.
6   Analyse and report findings.

The first step, writing the research question, can be challenging. It involves the process of determining what the organization needs to know to solve a problem. Because organizations are often in a hurry for answers, the temptation is to start the research process before analysing what information is needed. As a result, they may ask either a poorly defined research question or even the wrong question entirely. To be effective, research must be based on a question that is both well designed and narrowly focused. If the research question is too broad, too much information will be obtained. The large amount of resulting data will be difficult to analyse and, therefore, of little use to an organization. Even worse, if the wrong question is asked, useless information will be obtained, and all the research effort will be wasted.

Sources and participants

Researchers need to put considerable thought into planning the sources from which information can be obtained. The different sources for data are categorized as secondary and primary. Secondary data already exist because they have been collected by someone else. Primary data are collected by the researcher conducting their own research. In addition, secondary data can be categorized as internal, which the company already has, or external, which must be gathered from participants. In some cases, the answer to a research question might already be available as a result of research conducted by other organizations. Sometimes, an organization may already have enough internal data to answer the research question. If neither of these is true, then the researcher must design and conduct primary research.

A researcher will collect primary data directly from participants to answer a specific research question. Primary data are usually collected from a group of participants called a 'sample'. This sample consists of selected members from an entire group of individuals, which is called a 'population'. These selected members can be defined by demographic characteristics, such as age, gender, or occupation. They also might be defined by psychographic characteristics such as lifestyle. In addition, they can be defined by their geographic location or product usage levels. A description of the individuals in the sample is called the 'participant profile'. The method that will be used to choose the individuals to be included in a sample will differ depending on what type of research methodology will be used. Probability sampling is used to randomly select the people in a sample. Nonprobability sampling is utilized when the judgement of a researcher is used to make the selection.

There are four general criteria to consider when developing the detailed description, or participant profile, for either a qualitative or quantitative research study (Lee 2017). First, the researchers should decide what demographic characteristics are important. Then they will consider what psychographic characteristics should be considered. In addition, the importance of geographic location should be thought through.

Finally, for some research questions the potential subject's level of product use must be considered. The population being studied could be current customers who frequently purchase a product to determine how a company can improve that product's design. Past customers could be included in the sample to find sources of dissatisfaction or to determine what other competing products they also purchase. Rather than current or past customers, potential market segments of interest to that company can also be studied. For example, research can be conducted to determine what type of promotion might motivate older consumers to purchase. Another purpose of researching a sample of potential consumers is to determine how a product needs to be adapted to offer the features and benefits they desire. For example, a company that produces camping equipment might include in their sample individuals who are interested in extreme sports in order to learn how to adapt their product to meet these consumers' preferences.

Research approach

The next step is to choose a research approach. The process of conducting primary research starts with deciding whether the research question calls for descriptive or exploratory research. The choice will depend on whether or not a research question needs to be answered with quantifiable facts. If a research question asks 'Who?' 'How many?' or 'Which one?', descriptive research will be used. If a research question asks the question 'Why?', then exploratory research will be needed.

Understanding how an organization plans to use the information will help in making an appropriate decision. If an organization wishes to prove a fact about the demographic composition of its customers, such as how many females as compared to males purchase a product, then a descriptive study would be appropriate. If, on the other hand, an organization wishes to discover why sales are falling, it will need to conduct exploratory research.

Planning the research method

After choosing the research approach, researchers must then design the research method. This will include the details of how the research will be conducted, including when, where, and by whom. The available research methods will include surveys, focus groups, interviews, projective techniques, and observation. Online communication technology has resulted in an additional method referred to as mobile or virtual ethnography (Muskat, Muskat and Zehrer 2018).

A research plan will include the timeline for the research, the staff needed, and the budget. For example, this step may involve writing survey questions or the script to be used in a focus group. The more detailed the planning, the more smoothly the research will proceed. Therefore everything, from the layout of the survey form to who will be responsible for ensuring that the focus group participants arrive, should be considered.

Table 1.1 Research methods

Method	Description
Survey	Set of pre-determined questions
Focus groups	Group dynamics to draw out responses
Interviews	One-to-one in-depth discussion
Intercept interviews	Two to three short questions asked
Projective techniques	Creative techniques to get emotional responses
Observation	Watching people's behavior and actions
Virtual ethnography	Studying people in online communities

Conducting and reporting the research

Finally, researchers will be ready to conduct the research. Once done, the final task is for researchers to analyse the data and report the findings and conclusions. Analysis requires repeatedly going over the collected responses to find common themes, patterns, and connections. Reporting may be in the form of a written report, a verbal presentation, or both. A written report presenting the results of a quantitative research study will usually have an introduction followed by a description of the methodology. It will also have a section with findings supported with statistics and charts. These findings will be the basis of the recommendations given in the report. With quantitative research, someone who has not conducted the research can still write the report based on the findings.

A report for a qualitative research study will follow the same outline. However, because there are no statistics or charts, different types of visuals will be used to help explain the findings. Some tools that can be used include diagrams, quotes, photos, and even videos. With qualitative research, the person who conducted the research must be involved in the writing of the report.

Quantitative versus qualitative research

One of the questions that an organization must decide before conducting research is which research approach will be most appropriate. The approach chosen will depend on the research question and the type of information an organization is seeking. The two general research approaches are quantitative descriptive and qualitative exploratory. Each can be considered as being similar to a different type of toolbox. Each approach 'box' contains tools or methods that are most useful with that approach. After deciding the research approach, the company will choose the best method.

Table 1.2 Research studies and their use

Method	When to Use	How to Use
Quantitative	When details and numbers are needed, can be used to prove a hypothesis	Surveys on customer demographics or purchase frequency
Qualitative	When seeking insights on motivation/behaviour	Focus groups or other techniques on purchase motivation or desired benefits

Quantitative descriptive research

A company will perform descriptive research when it needs to obtain specific details on its consumers and their purchasing behaviour. Descriptive research is used when statistical data are needed on a fact. The tool used to conduct descriptive research is almost always surveys. The advantage of a survey is that, if the number of people surveyed, or sample, is large enough, it can be said that a fact has been proved with a certain percentage of certainty and the results can be applied to the entire group or population. Descriptive survey data can give answers such as '37 per cent of our customers is over the age of 55' or '52 per cent of our customers purchase four times a year'. If the number of people asked to complete the survey is large enough compared to the total population under study, the answer can even be said to have been proven.

Conducting descriptive research can be expensive and time-consuming depending on the number of participants. However, it is necessary if a company wants to prove or hypothesis about consumers or their behaviour. For example, a descriptive study can be designed to prove that '10 per cent of all current consumers will purchase the more expensive new product model'. This guess or hypothesis can be proved within a certain level of confidence that the answer obtained from the descriptive survey sample is true of the entire population. However, descriptive research can also be used to obtain details without relying on statistical proof. For example, a survey may be designed only to learn more about general consumer preferences.

Many organizations have relied heavily on surveys as their only means of market research. This is unfortunate as the type of information that surveys can provide is limited. It is difficult to get answers on underlying motivation or why a purchase is made as consumers are sometimes unaware of why they may decide.

Yet another reason for rethinking this dependence on descriptive surveys is that it is increasingly difficult to find enough people who are willing to respond. Because people are often pressed for time, and because of privacy issues, it is difficult to motivate people to respond to a survey by mail, email, or even in person. To make participating in a survey more convenient, social media is increasingly being used as a distribution method.

Qualitative exploratory research

Organizations should use exploratory research when a research question deals with finding information on consumer attitudes, opinions, and beliefs. Such exploratory research can be useful even when there is no specific problem to investigate. For example, an organization might use exploratory research to look for marketing opportunities by researching trends or changes in consumer behaviour, such as why they prefer to purchase. The research methods available to conduct exploratory studies include focus groups, interviews, projective techniques, and observation.

All the methods use a qualitative exploratory approach. Exploratory research is designed to let participants provide their own answers. The research question, rather than asking for facts, focuses on a consumer's needs, desires, preferences, and values. Because so many different answers will result, statistically provable answers cannot be generated. Exploratory qualitative studies, if designed with considerable thought as to what information is wanted and how it is to be obtained, can provide invaluable information to a company. Such a study may be large and complex or it can be conducted on a small scale. Either way, the consumer information received will provide details and insights that will help an organization adapt its product, price, promotion, and distribution to meet consumer desires.

When using exploratory research tools, the emphasis is not on the number of people who participate or the size of a sample. Instead, it is on choosing the correct participants and the analysis of the information they provide. For example, if asked why they purchase a company's product, even if everyone has a unique answer, common themes will almost always appear. A researcher will analyse the responses and then group them by these common themes. One advantage of qualitative research is that it can also be approached in low-cost ways that are available to even small businesses.

Combining methods

Sometimes the organization may develop a research plan that uses both approaches. For example, the organization may be faced with the situation of wanting to add new products, without being sure of what type would be desired. If they write a survey that provides as answers what they believe are possible ideas, they will limit the responses of participants. However, if they first conduct qualitative exploratory research using focus groups and interviews, they may find ideas that they had not considered. Then to ensure that the ideas are valid, the organization can develop and administer a quantitative survey.

New forms of research

Social media has provided new methods of conducting traditional research and entirely new research methods. One of the ways that social media can be used is to find research subjects. Because of its reach, subjects that cannot be contacted in traditional ways can now be invited to participate in a research study. In addition, social media can be used to post and distribute surveys. Finally, technology can be used to conduct focus groups and interviews without the research subjects being physically present.

The public's use of the organization's social media can also be used as a form of research itself. Social media analytics of the organization's sites can be used by researchers to learn more about who is using the organization's social media. Because such research is less expensive, more organizations are using online tools to analyse social media. They are relying less on traditional research methods (Barker 2020).

One use for online digital media research is to determine the answer to research questions. For example, an organization marketing a service may wish to learn what calls to action on their social media sites motivate a request for more information. Online messages on different benefits can be posted. One message might stress the upscale benefits of the service, while the other might promote its low cost. By analysing which call to action for more information is clicked most often, the organization can learn if luxury or cost-savings has more appeal.

Online communities are now also an opportunity for marketing research. These communities are groups of people who, while geographically distant, share an interest or lifestyle. These groups can now easily be contacted on social media to share ideas and opinions. If their interests are related to the organization's product, the researchers can go online and become part of the conversation. By doing so they will be able to better understand potential customers.

This approach can be used to obtain information about the behaviour of groups that might not be interested in participating in research. The researcher may silently observe the online conversation about favourite products, listening for relevant information. Another approach would be for the researcher to announce to the group that they are conducting research and ask permission to ask questions. Social media research can provide a rich source of insights not available from using other methods.

Social media marketing research

Social media provides new opportunities for conducting research on consumer insights using product reviews, social networking, and virtual ethnography, which is research of online communities. While it does not provide quantitative data to prove a hypothesis, social media marketing research can still be used to gain insight into consumer wants and needs. It is estimated that 80 per cent of social media posts contain personal opinions (Beaulac 2019).

First, online reviews of products and services can tell whether consumer expectations have been met. Social networking sites can also be used to determine trends in consumer preferences by following discussions about a product type to determine what is recommended. Analysis of product reviews can also make the organization aware of newly emerging competitors (Newton 2020). These can be found when the reviewer compares the company's product with another available on the market of which the organization is currently unaware. Such types of research are still being developed because new forms of social media are always being introduced.

Social media research has the advantage of being conducted in real time. If an organization is interested in following new trends in the marketplace, they can conduct a survey or focus group. The process will be faster if they simply monitor popular hashtags. Doing so will also allow them to monitor a larger audience than would be possible with other research techniques. Social media research can also be conducted at a much lower cost while at the same time reaching the products must dedicated users.

There are disadvantages in conducting social media research. The sample will not necessarily be representative of the population the organization wishes to study. In fact, it may be difficult to know anything about what is being studied. Such research also is not useful when in-depth information is needed from respondents. Because of the nature of social media communication, any responses will be brief.

While social media can be used to gain information from the public, it can also be used for competitive analysis of other organizations. Of course, the organization will want to monitor hashtags, online comments, and reviews of its own products. Competitive analysis is doing the same for other companies. By doing so the organization can learn consumer reactions to marketing strategies. It can also learn what consumers think about competing products. This information can then be used to improve the organization's own marketing and product development.

Virtual ethnography

One of the new uses of social media for research is virtual ethnography, which is a new form of traditional ethnography. In ethnography, the researcher travels to the location where the research participants are located to conduct research through observation. Such research is conducted with participants in a different country or from another culture. Not only are individuals studied but also the reactions between individuals and between individuals and the environment would be observed. With the development of technology, the idea of virtual ethnography developed. Rather than the research studying people who live in a specific location, the connection between individuals is studied while they are online, no matter their physical location. While some details as to how people look and react are lost, other less obvious relations may become apparent. Virtual ethnography can also be used to study relationships that take place online only as virtual relationships.

While research that examines download history and types and numbers of clicks is valid research, a researcher uses virtual ethnography to understand the reason why actions are taken. For example, a researcher might want to know whose opinions are considered valid when shared on a social networking site dedicated to a specific product. To do so they will first observe the online behaviour by reading or listening to the comments. They may then contact specific people who are on the site to ask questions about their behaviour.

Virtual ethnography requires an ability to analyse data but also the skill of the researcher in developing and handling online relationships with participants. First, the research question must be determined, which might be on the decision-making process of young professionals who are making the decision of which automobile to purchase. Once the question is formulated, the appropriate online community chosen must be found that the researcher will join. Perhaps there are online social groups of young professionals that discuss new car purchases. Next a schedule of interaction of when and how often the online discussions will be monitored must be developed. Learning about the behaviour of a group will take time. The researcher will then go online to both review current comments and to ask questions of community members.

Virtual ethnography research process

1   Decide research question.
2   Identify research subjects.
3   Find appropriate online community.
4   Listen and analyse conversations.
5   Guide conversation to obtain needed information.
6   Analyse the data.

A decision will need to be made as to whether the researcher will join the group by informing them of the purpose of the research or if they will simply join in the conversation noting interesting research findings as they occur. One of the advantages of publicly declaring the fact that researchers are conducting research is that they can steer the conversation to the research question. For example, a group of single, young professionals may not think of discussing how their automobile purchase decision will be affected if they were in a relationship. The researcher can ask if the decision process would be different. Whether the answer is yes or no, the online comments and conversations will provide insights into the thinking of the group members. Virtual ethnography is different from conducting surveys and interviews because it includes listening to ongoing conversations over time with the researcher as an active participant; the research is conducted as conversation rather than question and answer.

Discussion questions

1 Why is research considered an integral part of the marketing department's responsibility without which the company cannot succeed?
2 What is the difference between pure and applied research?
3 What is the difference between quantitative and qualitative research?
4 Why should even non-profit community organizations use marketing research?
5 What are the steps in the marketing research process?
6 How has social media expanded the means of conducting marketing research?

Answer these questions to start creating a marketing research plan

1 What qualitative methods can be used to better understand the organization's problem?
2 What quantitative methods can be used to answer the research question?
3 How to use social media to learn more about the research issue?

References

Barker, Matt. "Humanize the Data: Why Marketing Research is Having a Digital Reboot." *Marketing Week*. November 26, 2020. www.marketingweek.com/market-research-reboot-digital-focus/. Accessed March 15, 2021.

Beaulac, Hugh. "How to Use Social Media for Market Research." *CXL*. February 18, 2019. https://cxl.com/blog/social-media-market-research/. Accessed February 2, 2021.

Lee, Kuan-Huei. "Conceptual Foundation of Consumer Behavior." *The Routledge Handbook of Consumer Behaviour in Hospitality and Tourism*. 2017. Ed. Saurabh Kumar Dixit. Abingdon, Oxon: Routledge.

Muskat, Birgit, Matthias Muskat and Anita Zehrer. "Qualitative Interpretive Mobile Ethnography." *Anatolia*, 2018, 29: 98–107.

Newton, Stephanie. "Why Online Reviews are Important for Every Business." *Brand Watch*. September 4, 2020. www.brandwatch.com/blog/why-online-reviews-are-important-for-every-business/. Accessed January 22, 2021.

Zimmerman, Steve. "Community Influences: Understanding Nonprofit Markets." *Nonprofit Quarterly*. July 31, 2018. https://nonprofitquarterly.org/community-influences-understanding-nonprofit-markets/. Accessed February 20, 2021.

2 Developing a hypothesis and research question

Hypothesis

The term 'hypothesis' is used when a research attempts to determine if something is true. Hypothesis is simply a statement of fact written by researchers. A quantitative method, such as a survey, is then used to generate statistics based on responses. Of course, because only a sample, rather than everyone will participate in the research, it is impossible to absolutely prove that a hypothesis is true. However, conducting quantitative research and then analysing the results will answer the question with a specific percentage of certainty. Because there is a wealth of data online, hypothesis can be used to narrow the focus of the research. It may seem counter-intuitive, but more data is not better (Johnson 2020). Obtaining too much information can lead to mental fatigue and as a result a return to making decisions based on already conceived assumptions.

A hypothesis is a deduction that is made by the company or individuals commissioning the research. Perhaps an academic publisher has come up with an idea for a new textbook that can be easily read on a smartphone. The question is whether they should spend the money to develop and introduce the product. Qualitative research has indicated that many students would be interested in this product. However, the finance department of the company has stated that at least 20 per cent of students who currently want to purchase the textbook will need to purchase the new product to cover development costs and make it financially viable.

This first hypothesis is the null hypothesis and will be stated as what the company does not wish to be true. (The symbol H_0 is used to designate the null hypothesis.) The null hypothesis is considered true until proven false. For the publisher in this example the null hypothesis is that less than 20 per cent of students will be interested in purchasing the product. The alternative hypothesis would be that 20 per cent or more of students will be interested in purchasing the product. (The alternative hypothesis is designated H_1.)

DOI: 10.4324/9781003165194-3

One hypothesis is the opposite of the other and so both cannot be true. A quantitative survey will then need to be conducted to test the hypotheses.

This is an example of a simple hypothesis. It only contains three elements: the population (students), the variable (new product), and the outcome (sales). A complex hypothesis adds more variables to the question. The company may want to know how pricing will affect the sales of the new product. So, this may be added to the research question, which becomes more complex because now two variables are involved. First, are students going to buy the product and, secondly, how does price affect this decision.

The statistical tests cannot be used to prove the hypothesis true. This is impossible as the only way to know with 100 per cent accuracy if a hypothesis is true is to survey the entire population. If the null hypothesis is proved false, then the alternative hypothesis (that 20 per cent or more of students will be interested) can be accepted as being true. The null hypothesis needs to be expressed in such a way that its rejection leads to the acceptance of the preferred conclusion – developing the new product.

Reasons for conducting research

There are several different issues that an organization can choose to research. Research on the consumer marketplace can be used to determine what group of consumers is buying a specific product. Companies can also consider conducting research regarding competitors' products and services as it can provide valuable information on how products can improve. Organizations should analyse their own customers' perception of competitors, as such research helps to determine whether companies should add to their own products any of the benefits provided by competing products.

Table 2.1 Sample research problems, objectives, and questions

Problem	Objective	Question
Bakery is located in a deteriorating neighbourhood	To determine if the bakery should relocate	What percent of potential customers are lost because of the bakery's location?
Our restaurant has a new competition opening in town	To determine how to keep existing market share	What promotion should be used in communicating the restaurant's unique menu?
Our clothing company needs a new source of revenue	To determine if there is a potential market segment for a new line of clothing aimed at the elderly	What is the right marketing mix that will motivate older people to purchase new clothing?

Another use of market research is to determine the composition of the current customer segment including demographic factors such as age, income level, and education. Market research can examine customers' motivation for purchasing a product. Distribution research is conducted to determine if the product is being sold at the right locations. This would include the right store location but also if the consumer prefers to purchase online. Another important area of research is determining if a product is being effectively promoted, including both the marketing message and the media through which it is communicated. Lastly, determining the correct price for a new product can make the difference between a successful and unsuccessful product launch. Information gathered on all of these issues will help businesses to learn where and how they need to improve their marketing strategy.

Possible research issues

- Composition of customer market segment.
- Consumers' perception of competition.
- Motivation for purchase.
- Determine what sites are used.
- Improvement of product.
- Effectiveness of different messages and media.
- Ease of purchase.
- Correct pricing levels.

Research question

A problem can be described as a question for which there is currently no answer. When faced with a problem, it is tempting for an organization to start researching the answer immediately. The temptation to begin researching right away results from the belief that an organization both understands the source of the problem and considers that the answer is self-evident. However, time will not be saved if a company starts to research immediately. Instead, both time and money will be wasted, as the first analysis of a problem is rarely correct.

This decision to start research without proper planning is a common mistake made by all types of organizations (Agee 2009). Unfortunately, a company that starts to research prematurely has probably not even correctly identified the source of a problem much less its possible solution. This failure will lead to one of the most frequent mistakes in marketing research, which is to base the research study on the wrong research question. If this is done, the original problem will remain even if the research is conducted correctly because the researchers asked the wrong question.

Writing a research question that clearly states the problem to be researched takes considerable thought. Since this question is the rationale for the all research that will be conducted, it is well worth the effort to make sure that the question is focused on the correct problem. A well-written research question will make planning the remainder of the research study much easier. There is a relationship between the specific problem and the resulting research question.

Examples of problems and research questions

* Declining market share: How can we motivate purchases by older consumers?
* Reduced marketing budget: What social media do our customers use?
* Decline in non-profit funding: Why do our contributors donate?
* Determining location: Where do our customers currently shop?

It is sometimes thought that once a question has been written, this step in the process is completed. Because determining the correct question will ultimately affect the type of study that is conducted, considerable thought and reflection are necessary. The question might even evolve once the research is underway as the population is better understood. This may result from learning that the initial assumptions on which the question was based were wrong. Good research starts with data, which are turned into information to provide organizations with the knowledge they need to solve problems. For research to be useful, researchers must understand a company's problem, and not just have an understanding of research methodology.

Research issues may be expressed with questions that start with 'Why?' or 'How?', such as 'Why have young people stopped purchasing our soft drinks?' or 'How can we use online promotion to regain our market share of young soft drink consumers?'. These will most likely result in an exploratory research approach that is qualitative. This is because researchers do not have enough information to state the question more narrowly. Therefore, they may anticipate that many different answers from participants will result and that the answers may vary greatly.

Research issues may also be expressed with questions that start with 'What?', 'Who?', or 'How many?'. Questions such as 'What is the most popular soft drink among university students?', 'Who is the purchase decision maker in families when soft drinks are bought?', and 'How many consumers are willing to pay more to have our product sold in recycled bottles?' are all questions that will result in descriptive, quantitative research. Researchers should never first decide the type of research methodology and then phrase the question to justify its use. Instead, the research methodology should be determined by the type of question.

Rules for writing research questions

There are general rules that should be remembered when a research question is written. First, the question should be an assertion of fact on which the researcher takes a side. It should not be stated in vague terms such as 'The reason for declining sales may be a lack of promotion'. The purpose of the research will be to determine if it is or if it isn't. Therefore, the researcher must decide which way to state the question because it can't be both ways.

In addition, the researcher must state the question so that it argues only one point of fact. The question 'Are sales declining because of a lack of promotion or because of increased competition?' is two research questions. Different methodologies and different research participants may be needed for each. If the researcher tries to combine them, the research may answer neither question.

Lastly, a research question must pass the 'So what?' test. Does the question generate enough interest from management that they will be willing to approve the research? The answer must lead to a recommendation that will either significantly increase revenue or decrease expenses, or it will not be approved.

Research questions can be developed for any component of the marketing mix and, also, the target market segment and consumer behaviour. For both quantitative and qualitative studies, the question itself needs to be as narrowly defined as possible. To do so, researchers must define who, where, what, when, and how, as will be used in the question.

Defining the research question

- Who? Participants who will take part in the research.
- Where? Geographic location of current or potential consumers.
- When? Time frame of the behaviour under study.
- What? Specific description of the product.
- Why? Attitude or motivation of concern to researchers.
- How? Proposed actions that could be undertaken by the company.

Cross-cultural research challenges

International marketing research can be defined as research that is conducted in one or more countries other than the country of the company commissioning the research. This international research may be conducted because this company already sells products in more than one country or because they hope to do so in the future. If more than one country is involved in the research project, the company may decide to conduct the research either simultaneously or sequentially, country by country.

When researching the introduction of an existing product into a new country, any company needs to understand the unique needs, wants, and desires of the potential customers. Companies will use this information to adjust the products, prices, distribution, and promotion to make their products more attractive to local consumers. Rather than adapt a current product, companies may also use marketing research because they want to develop new products that uniquely meet the needs of consumers in other countries. In this case, research is even more important.

Almost all international marketing research is also cross-cultural research (Hofstede 2001). This is true because national boundaries are usually also cultural boundaries. Marketing researchers need to be aware that within any additional country, there may be more than one cultural group. Therefore, marketing research designed for another country may need to be adjusted for more than one culture.

Cross-cultural research at home

Cross-cultural research may also need to be conducted in a company's own country. This will be the case if the country where a company is based is home to more than one cultural group. These different cultural groups may have existed together in the same country for centuries. Alternatively, different cultural groups may result from recent immigration.

Unfortunately, just because there is more than one cultural group living in a country does not mean that market researchers are adept or even aware of the need to adjust their methodology. This lack of awareness may result because the newest immigrant groups are usually not represented in the ranks of marketing professionals. Of course, this fact will change over time as newer immigrant groups and their families become more familiar with the majority cultural group. However, the lower education level that currently exists explains why there are few marketing professionals. As a result, this population might be ignored when conducting marketing research. Unfortunately, by not adapting marketing research techniques to better assess the wants and needs of immigrant groups, marketers are ignoring a potential consumer segment.

Unique research questions

The marketing research process does not change because it is being conducted across cultures. What does change is the choice of methodology and how that methodology is implemented. In addition, marketing across cultures may result in unique research questions. For example, aspects of consumer behaviour that researchers take for granted in their own culture may need to be researched in another. Design preferences such as colour, style, and package size may also change from culture to culture. The preferred brand name may vary as well. In addition, where a product is purchased and how that product is used may differ. These variations will result in the need to ask additional research questions.

Translation issues

Another issue is that companies must translate all research material. Translation of both verbal and written information may be needed during several steps in the research process. This includes the planning phase, when preparing research materials and putting together a final report. There are now many software tools that will translate between languages. However, the meaning of the question can change dramatically with only one word not being translated correctly. The best way to approach this task is for researchers and translators to work as a collaborative team to review the translated material for accuracy and meaning (Cincan 2016).

Levels of cultural difference

When developing a research plan for conducting international research marketing, researchers should consider the level of cultural dissimilarity between a company's home country and the new geographic area in which it plans to market. These differences could include both language differences and cultural values or dimensions. Sometimes research conducted in the same country as where a company is located might still be faced with different language and cultural values issues when researching consumers from a minority cultural group. While the considerations of language and cultural values must still be considered, this research will be easier to undertake. This is because even if they are not members of a culture, researchers will probably have been exposed to that culture through personal relationships or through the media. In addition, finding assistance in obtaining cultural information will be easier as local experts can be found to assist with research.

'Self-reference' is a term used to describe the fact that everyone believes his or her way of life is the 'norm'. This is not necessarily a problem unless a person meets other people who have different ideas of what constitutes 'normal' behaviour. This person then has the choice of feeling threatened and reacting negatively or reacting with interest and exploring the cultural difference.

When researching marketing issues across cultures, it is imperative for researchers to remember that the self-reference criterion is unacceptable.

Instead, researchers must remain aware that all consumers have their behaviour and desires shaped by their national and ethnic culture. Even within a single country several different ethnic and cultural differences may exist among people who belong to different groups.

Research proposal

The research process starts when management becomes aware of a general problem. After all, companies do not conduct pure research just for the sake of 'knowing'. The problem may become apparent because revenue is negatively impacted due to falling sales. Management may become aware of negative comments about the company or product on social media. Both cases suggest there is a problem but do not provide enough information in order to correct what is being done wrong. On the positive side, a problem might involve the need to research how to promote a new product that will lead to increased profit. After management, along with researchers, defines the general problem, the research objective will be stated. Finally, a more specific research question will be asked.

Any organization contemplating conducting research should start by analysing internal data to help clarify the issue that is causing concern and then should formulate a research question. Once the decision has been made that primary research needs to be conducted to answer the research question, the organization should write their research proposal. Writing such a proposal would be a requirement for someone working in a marketing research company. In this case, the proposal will be a formal document that includes all details of the proposed research, along with staff assignments, a timeline for completion, and a budget with cost estimates. A marketing research firm should spend considerable effort in writing such proposals as they form the basis for contracts between marketing research firms and client companies. For large corporations, a research proposal will be written internally and then sent to management for approval.

However, it is also recommended that small businesses and non-profit organizations planning to conduct research should first write a proposal. In this case the document is for internal use as an informal contract and planning guide. If there is a concern raised during the research process regarding the cost of conducting research, this proposal will remind everyone concerned of the commitment agreed upon. The proposal also serves as a basis for allocating tasks and assigning responsibility within organizations. The time that is spent on writing a proposal will be saved later when there is no need to renegotiate resources. A well-written research proposal will answer any questions that management, other employees, or board members might have about the research that is to be conducted.

Table 2.2 Proposal Outline

Section	Contents
Problem	Introduction Research objective Research question
Methodology	Research approach Research method Data collection plan
Analysis and Findings	Data analysis Methods of reporting findings
Appendices	Budget and timeline Examples of research tools Confidentiality statement

Reasons for writing a research proposal

The proposal describes a plan of action or the 'map' of what is to be accomplished. Second, it is the basis of a contract. A research proposal ensures that everyone agrees on what is to be accomplished, at an estimated cost, and with the necessary resources. Third, it is a method of accountability that can be used to keep research on track.

Too often managers use research to find data to support a decision they have already made, rather than finding information to help decide (Stobierski 2019). The process of writing a research proposal will help clarify management's thinking. Another reason is that the proposal might be required by the company commissioning the research.

Proposal components

A research proposal is essentially a 'game plan' of what will be done. It can vary in length from a single page to as many as 20 pages, depending on the size and complexity of a research project. Regardless of the length, a proposal should at least consist of three sections plus an appendix.

The first section is an introduction that describes a problem and states the research objective and research question. The second section describes the research objection, including the methodology, research approach, method, and data collection plan. A description of how the sample of participants will be chosen will also be included. The section on analysis and findings will contain information on how the data will be analysed and how the findings will be reported. Finally the appendices will contain detailed information on the budget, personnel needs, timeline, and other relevant information.

The introduction of the proposal describes the background to a problem and the rationale for undertaking research. The information used to define this problem will have already been obtained through internal secondary research and through interviewing relevant company personnel. This first section of the proposal will describe the research objective and research question. The introduction will also include information on who is the author of the proposal and who will be conducting the research. It will state under whose authority the proposal is being submitted. The proposal starts with this information to provide legitimacy to its contents.

The research objective will start with a description of what is currently known about the problem under consideration. This description would result from information obtained through internal secondary research that was conducted by researchers before writing a research proposal. Internal information, such as financial and sales data, would assure readers the research question was based on accurate assumptions. This section provides the justification for the research.

The second section of the proposal will then explain the research methodology, including the approach and method that will be used to answer the research question and the data collection plan. It should not be assumed that those reading the proposal are familiar with research terms and methods. Therefore, when discussing the methodology, it is important that a proposal both explains and clarifies the meaning of any terms as these words might be used differently by managers. If researchers suggest that research should be conducted with more than one approach and method, it is especially important for a proposal to explain the reasons for doing so.

Once an approach has been explained, a written proposal should provide as much information as possible about the method. The more thoroughly a research method is detailed, the more management will feel confident in approving the proposal. In addition, the more planning that is done before the start of the research, the easier the research will be to conduct.

If a proposal suggests focus groups be conducted, the proposal should state the number of focus groups, who the participants will be, and the topics to be discussed. In addition, it should also explain how many people will participate and how they will be chosen. Logistical details such as dates, times, and locations should be given. Finally, the choice of moderator for the focus group should be discussed.

When research involves conducting descriptive quantitative research such as surveys, proposals should include information on both their method and the participants. This would include information on the length of the survey and the type of questions to be asked. Proposals should also describe the procedure for testing survey forms. Information on sampling plans and how participants will be chosen should also be included. Finally, how researchers will analyse the data should be discussed.

The final section on analysis and findings will describe how the data will be analysed and reported. This section would include information on how the coding of transcripts or notes from focus groups will be used to find common responses and themes. It would also include how survey data will be analysed, including any software packages that will be used.

A proposal should be very specific on what information will be provided to management and in what format. The research deliverables might include not just a final report but also ongoing feedback. This might be done informally through phone calls and email. Management may be offered regularly scheduled meetings and weekly reports during the research process. The more research the cost of the research, the more management will want to be kept abreast of progress. This is also helpful for researchers as any misunderstandings can be clarified and rectified immediately, rather than having disappointed clients at the end of the process when it is too late to make changes to the methodology.

Any final material contained in the appendices of a research proposal could include a breakdown of costs, personnel needs, a time schedule for completion, examples of the research methods, and any technical details of the data analysis technique. It is important that a detailed timeline be provided in the research proposal, as it is not unusual for management to not understand that good research takes time. A proposal should provide a breakdown of when each task will be completed.

The appendices should contain a statement of confidentiality. This statement would explain that any information about a company discussed during meetings with researchers will be kept confidential. In addition, a proposal must state whether the research methodology created to conduct the research belongs to the marketing research firm concerned or the company commissioning the research. Lastly, what will happen to all resulting documentation will be explained.

Discussion questions

1   Why marketing research cannot prove a hypothesis to be true?
2   Why is developing the research question the most important step in the research process?
3   What are the issues that make it more difficult to conduct research in other countries?
4   What are the reasons for writing a research proposal before starting research?
5   What are the unique challenges when conducting cross-cultural research?

6   What are the components of a research proposal?
7   Why should the research proposal be careful to explain marketing research terms?

Answer these questions to continue creating a marketing research plan

1   What is the research objective?
2   What is the research question?
3   Can it be stated as a hypothesis?
4   Are there unique challenges because of differing cultures?

References

Agee, Jane. "Developing Qualitative Research Questions: A Reflective Process." *International Journal of Qualitative Studies in Education*, 2009, 22(4): 431–447.

Cincan, Alina. "Challenges in Translating Surveys." *In Box Translation*. May 4, 2016. https://inboxtranslation.com/blog/challenges-translating-surveys/. Accessed February 23, 2021.

Hofstede, Geert. *Culture's Consequences: Comparing Values, Behaviours, Institutions and Organizations across Cultures*. 2001. London: SAGE.

Johnson, Gregg. "Is Your Marketing Strategy Based on the Right Data?" *Harvard Business Review*. May 14, 2020. https://hbr.org/2020/05/is-your-marketing-strategy-based-on-the-right-data#. Accessed March 14, 2021.

Stobierski, Tim. "The Advantages of Data Driven Decision Making." *Harvard Business Review*. August 26, 2019. https://online.hbs.edu/blog/post/data-driven-decision-making. Accessed April 24, 2021.

3 Conducting secondary research

Types of data

After a researcher has defined the research problem, the next step in the research process is to determine what external information is already available that could assist in answering the research question. The two types of external research data that can be obtained by market researchers are commonly called 'secondary' and 'primary'. A researcher will obtain primary data directly from research participants. In contrast, secondary data already exist as someone else has collected the information as the result of previous research. Secondary data, despite the name, are the first type of data that should be analysed by researchers. Since secondary data already exist, obtaining this information is less costly than obtaining primary data. Not only do researchers not have to spend the money to conduct research but using secondary research data also saves time. Finding information is much easier and quicker than in the past, as there is a wealth of online sources of secondary data. In fact, the amount of available data is so great that researchers need to develop skills in determining what information is relevant and credible. The business or organization will already have sources of internal data that are often overlooked (Boyd 2019). Sales data and customer complaints can be particularly useful when developing the research question. The secondary data found online may have been collected as part of research conducted by an academic institution, a government department, or a trade association. Additional sources are searches on social media sites or a commercial data provider.

The faculties of academic institutions such as colleges and universities may conduct research that has been funded by a grant. This grant may have been received from a large corporation that needed research data on consumer preferences or from a government agency that wanted information on social trends. If the grant was from a corporation, the data may not be available to the public. Research funded by the government will be available

DOI: 10.4324/9781003165194-4

to be used by other researchers. Research may also be undertaken solely as the result of professorial interest. Since the goal of professors is to publish research, this kind of data will be made available to the public.

Government agencies will also conduct their own research to provide information to guide policy decisions. The information collected will include population demographics and economic trends, all of which should be available to researchers. In addition, trade associations will conduct research on products produced by members of the association. For example, the automobile manufacturers association in many countries gathers information on auto industry-related statistics, such as the popularity of electric vehicles. Therefore, primary research on the auto industry should not be conducted without first ascertaining what secondary data are already available.

A newer source of secondary data is social media. While the purpose of these sites is not to collect data, all the comments, reviews, likes, photos, and videos that discuss consumer products and trends can be treated as a source of secondary data. Finally, commercial research companies will provide data for a fee. Not using at least some of these already available sources of information is wasteful of the researchers' financial and time resources.

Benefits of using secondary data

Once a research proposal has been approved, researchers may be tempted to immediately start conducting the primary research methodology by conducting a survey or holding a focus group. However, there are many benefits to first conducting external secondary research. These benefits include lower costs, research answers, assistance with the design of research methodology, and providing industry information.

The costs and time involved in obtaining primary data include determining and obtaining a sample, designing the research methodology, and analysing the findings. Because secondary data, unlike primary data, have already been collected, they can be obtained at lower cost. However, not all secondary data are free. If the data are obtained from a commercial provider, there may be a cost involved. If this is the case researchers may find that the cost of the secondary data is still lower than the cost of obtaining the data through primary research.

There are occasions when only secondary research is conducted. By analysing the secondary data, researchers might find the answer to their research question. This is most likely to happen if the research question is general in nature. For example, if the research question is the percentage of people in the city who are concerned about weight gain, these data might have already been collected by a local health organization. However, most research questions are more specific to a company's product or target market segment, and the data collected through secondary research data will not be specific enough to provide the necessary answers.

Even if it does not answer the research question, another benefit of secondary research is that it can provide information that will help to design the primary research methodology (Shapiro 2018). Data from existing sources of consumer preference can provide information on desired product benefits that will help in the design of a survey or focus group questions. For example, if a company is considering designing a new accessory for use with cell phones, research of studies conducted on cell phone design might find an industry study on consumer preferences regarding features. In addition, comments on social networking and product review sites will provide comments on current products and preferred benefits. This information could then be used to develop a survey that could be used with current or potential customers.

Another benefit of secondary research is that it can provide background information on an industry. Even if the secondary data that are analysed do not directly provide the answer to the problem, their collection and analysis are still helpful in providing background information and context on the research issue. Using this knowledge can help a researcher choose the correct research method and design a better research tool.

Secondary data requirements

Secondary research for existing data is always the first choice for researchers as it saves time and money. However, secondary data should only be used if the data are relevant and relate appropriately to the problem. The data should also be credible, timely, accurate, and affordable. Ensuring the usability of secondary data is the responsibility of researchers.

Data used by the researcher should not only deal with the appropriate consumer market segment or the product category but also be relevant by specifically addressing what researchers need to know. With vast amounts of information available online, it is relatively easy to find data. However, researchers must take the time and effort to verify the credibility of sources of data to ensure these come from reputable organizations or publications. If the source is a website, it can be more difficult to determine creditability. Researchers must verify which individual or organization is responsible for the content of a website.

Besides the relevance and credibility of a source, researchers should determine the date when a study was published, as the data should be timely. What is considered outdated depends on the product or consumer groups being studied. Fashion and technology information becomes dated very quickly. In other fields, the opposite is true.

Table 3.1 Secondary research process

Steps	Tasks
Conduct internal secondary research	Internal data
	Company personnel
Conduct external secondary research	Customer-focused publications
	Academic studies
	Business publications
	Government data sources
If answer to research question found	Write report
If answer not found	Propose and conduct primary research

When evaluating the accuracy of data, a researcher should ascertain who it was who originally collected the data included in a study. It is not necessary to know researchers personally, but it is necessary to know that the specific organization for which researchers collected the data is reputable. How the data were collected should also be examined. Data that have been collected using the wrong method or a flawed sample will result in erroneous results. Finally, the cost of the data should be considered. Even the best data cannot be used if they cannot be afforded.

Sources of data

Quantitative secondary data are numerical information on the external environment, industry, and consumers that already exist. Most of this information will be from statistical studies conducted by academic institutions, trade associations, government agencies, or marketing research firms. Researchers will find numerous sources of information on the external environment and consumers. However, they may also discover that finding statistical data on competitors can be challenging. In this case qualitative secondary data that are not statistical can be gathered from sources such as websites, magazines, and newspapers that can be found online. This type of information is very important when researching consumer preferences and competitors.

Sometimes secondary data may be the end of the research process (Fuld 2019). The research question may be whether to introduce a new product to the marketplace. Secondary data on competitors may reveal that other companies have tried and failed with a similar product. Unless the company's product has a compelling difference, the research question is answered negatively and the process stops.

Internal data

Researchers can obtain existing information by analysing internal company data. In addition, they can interview company personnel who have relevant information about the problem. All companies have at least some available data that can be used by researchers. For example, data gathered in useable form as the result of previous research may already exist. The marketing department in a larger company usually routinely conducts consumer research when developing new products or new promotion campaigns. Smaller companies should not just address customer comments and complaints, they should be maintained (Arline 2019). These research data would be kept in a marketing information database so that they would then be available to assist in answering future research questions.

Also available to the researcher are raw data that come from other departments in a company. For example, even small companies have sales receipts that researchers can use to learn where their customers live. In addition, customer complaint forms will provide useful information on product improvement ideas. A company's financial records will also give information on sales activity by time and region. If a company is large enough to have a customer database, the data it contains will provide information on customers' purchase habits. Data on product service requests can provide insights into possible design problems, while catalogue orders display information on customers' geographic location. Finally, website hits will let a company know how many people are accessing the information. In fact, companies may have a significant amount of internal data already that could be analysed.

Table 3.2 Sources of internal secondary data

Information	Source
Existing data	Sales receipts
	Customer complaint information
	Customer databases
	Product service requests
	Catalogue orders
	Website hits
Company personnel	Sales force
	Production managers
	Financial analysts
	Human resources professionals

Quantitative secondary data

Most external quantitative secondary data result from statistical survey research that has been already conducted. Common sources of this data are academic institutions where professors conduct statistical research. In addition, trade associations will collect statistical data for their members. Local or federal government offices collect data as part of the services they provide, while commercial research firms collect statistical data to sell. These organizations have the financial and staff resources to be able to conduct a survey with a large enough sample to ensure that data are statistically valid. Academic and government data are often available to a researcher at no cost. Trade association data are usually available only to member organizations and commercial research data must be purchased.

The secondary data that result from studies conducted by academic researchers can most often be found published in academic journals. However, often the studies are basic and not applied research. While such data may provide the researcher with insights into the causes of a problem, they will rarely answer a research question directly. However, examining the research of others can provide information on some basic questions.

The secondary data compiled by trade associations are usually specifically focused on the consumers who purchase a product, such as orange juice or women's fashions, sold by member companies. This information can provide very specific and therefore valuable data on consumption trends and changes in consumer preferences. However, because detailed information on consumer preferences would be helpful to competitors selling substitute products, this information may only be available to those companies that belong to the association. Less sensitive data on consumption trends may be available to the general public on the association's website.

Government departments and offices usually collect data on social trends or issues. These data are almost always available to the general public and can be accessed directly on websites. Each government office will be responsible for conducting studies in their area of concern. For example, in the United States, the Department of Commerce conducts studies on business activity in different regions of the country. Likewise in Europe, the European Union website can be searched for industry information.

Since social media posts are in the public domain, they can be a rich source of information. This can be done informally by simply going online and reading. However, a more systematic approach would be using online applications that monitor, track, gather, and analyse comments. These might be comments about the researcher's organization, but such data can also be used to analyse consumer comments about competitors. Marketing research firms are also a source of quantitative secondary data. These companies specialize in researching a certain product category or consumer market segment on a continual basis. These data are then available for purchase by any interested company or individual.

Qualitative secondary data

Qualitative secondary data are also available to researchers. Qualitative sources such as general newspapers and magazines are sometimes overlooked by market researchers as sources of information on consumer choices and competing products. These types of publications are often aimed at consumers who belong to a specific demographic group or consume specific types of products. These lifestyle publications, which can be found online, are particularly useful for consumer marketing research.

Many magazines are written to appeal to a specific demographic group. For example, a magazine entitled *Retirement Living* would be read by people who are either already retired or who are still employed but planning their retirement. If marketing researchers were interested in what types of issues are of concern to this group, examining the table of contents from several issues of the magazine would help to provide this information. A travel company may also notice that many issues of the magazine had articles that addressed the new trend of grandparents traveling with grandchildren. These data could be used to develop new types of tour packages.

Other publications are aimed at groups of people who share a specific psychographic interest or lifestyle. There are magazines aimed at sports enthusiasts and ones aimed at people who engage in specific hobbies. Market researchers in any industry should make a habit of reviewing publications aimed at their customers to keep abreast of consumer trends. These lifestyle magazines would also provide valuable information to market researchers in related industries such as hobby supply stores. Even advertisements can be a source of data. If a certain type of car accessory is being heavily promoted, such as heated cup holders, then eventually consumers will be looking for this product and stores should have them in stock.

Magazines and newspapers that cover business subjects are also a source of qualitative secondary data. They will often carry articles that relate to new consumer interests or product trends. Trade publications will also focus on a single product or industry. These business publications should be received by marketing departments and kept on file for research purposes. Likewise, any trade publications pertaining to specific industry trends should be received regularly so that appropriate trade association publications will be readily available in a marketing department along with competitors' catalogues and other promotional material.

Many websites devoted to groups that share a specific interest also contain information that is pertinent. Blogs, chatrooms, and social networking websites are easy ways to research consumer interests, particularly those of younger consumers. Social networking sites that allow people to post reviews of products and services can provide valuable insights.

When considering the cause of a problem that is being researched, it is important to consider the actions of a company's competitors. A large corporation might have an established system for gathering information on competitors' new products, promotions, or new target market segments. However, even small companies can keep abreast of competitor actions. It is not enough to consider only direct competitors (Cote 2020). Instead, competitors would be any company that sells a product that provides a similar benefit. Because new products are always being introduced as society encounters new problems, this type of analysis must be done on a continual basis.

Other sources of qualitative secondary data

Besides the usual sources of quantitative and qualitative data available to track competitor actions, researchers may need to take a more creative approach to find the required information. Marketing researchers should obviously routinely read all types of newspapers and magazines that focus on business issues to learn about competitors. However, other methods will also be needed because not all the relevant information will be published. Here, observation of competitors should be considered. For example, the owners of a sporting goods equipment store might visit other similar stores to find which type of products is being carried at other stores. Watching sporting events would provide information on what brands of equipment are popular at different skill levels. In addition, useful information can be obtained by visiting competing companies or places where competitor products are sold.

Another source is to use marketing studies conducted by other companies or organizations. While companies may not be willing to share the recommendations that arose from the studies, they may be willing to share their raw data either freely or for a price. If it is possible, the ethical issues must be considered. The research study participants may not agree to have the information shared with others. While useful, the data may not be a substitute for primary research as every consumer situation is unique (Hemsley 2017). Instead, it should be considered a first step to conducting primary research.

Valuable information can also be gathered through networking. If funds allow, researchers should attend trade association events so they can network and hear the latest industry news. In addition, researchers will hear all the informal gossip regarding those competitors who are thinking of introducing new products or promotions. If trade shows are not possible, all businesspeople can afford to network in the community by attending local business meetings and events. At such events a researcher might find them in conversation with a local media representative who might know about the future promotion plans of competitors or the local business reporter who should have the latest news about new products being introduced by competitors. Even real estate agents are sources of information, as they will have information on what companies are looking for new space because of expansion plans.

Uses of secondary data

Three major issues that a marketing researcher should use secondary research to explore are the external environment, the industry, and consumer segments. Fortunately, much of this research can be conducted right from a researcher's computer. Research on the external environment should include searching for data on social, economic, legal, and technological issues that might affect the research question. When researching the external environment, the secondary research might focus on social changes that could affect the benefits that consumers desire from a product. Another example of research on the external environment would be general economic news, as this would affect the pricing of a product. Researchers might examine the legal environment for changes in laws that could affect how a product may be packaged and promoted. Finally, the technological environment needs to be researched for any implications it may have on new product development. Online sites that discuss and review new tech products would be particularly helpful.

Secondary research could also gather information on an entire industry to see if there are changes that might affect a research question. These would include general data on changes and trends in that industry. In the case of the dessert product, data might reveal a trend towards smaller portion sizes or packaging that will go directly from the microwave to the table. A final issue to be researched might be competing products. A researcher will need to know if there are new competing dessert products that consumers are purchasing.

One last general issue that might need to be researched would be information on consumer segments. This secondary research could be on the current market segment or on a new potential market segment. For example, the current market segment targeted by the company for their product might be families. In this case research should focus on any changes in food consumption patterns for families. Research might reveal that families are serving less sweet desserts because of health concerns. A researcher might also focus on new target market segments, such as young single professionals and their dessert preferences.

Combining secondary and primary data

Researchers will need to understand how to use secondary research to design primary research. For example, a researcher may be presented with the problem of declining sales of fruit juice products. One of the first questions they would want answered is whether juice consumption is declining or whether it is just that the company's product is not being purchased.

Conducting a statistically valid study of all juice drinkers in a country is possible but would be an expensive and time-consuming effort. Fortunately, such as study is not necessary if secondary data are available. This data may have been collected by a government department of agriculture or a health association of an industry group.

Using these sources, a researcher will be able to learn whether people are still drinking juice. If the answer is that juice consumption is on the rise, the company's declining sales must be due to consumers buying other brands. Further external research would include reading trade publications on the beverage industry. Here it should be learned that juice is not being given as prominent a shelf space in local grocery stores because of all the new health drinks on the market. This knowledge gives the researcher a good indication of what the problem might be.

However, the secondary quantitative and qualitative data do not answer the question as to whether the lack of shelf space is the problem for their product. A research question or hypothesis is then developed that consumers do not notice the juice display and therefore are not motivated to purchase. The researcher can now design a primary research study to obtain data on whether this hypothesis is true.

Secondary data are also useful in designing qualitative studies. To use the same juice example, researchers may want to know more about how and when people drink. Secondary research using online social media sources would provide information on trends. For example, following comments on social media sites concerned with health, can provide insights into how people view the benefits. Reviewing information on social media sites that provides ideas for entertaining may provide information on juice is used in cocktails. These ideas can then be further explored in a focus group.

Cross-cultural data analysis

Much of the secondary data that a marketing researcher might find available in the United States or Europe may not be available in all countries. The availability of information on demographics and consumer behaviour depends on having an institution gathering and maintaining the data over time.

This continuity, in turn, depends on having a stable government or nongovernmental bureaucracy to support that institution.

Another issue when conducting international secondary research is that many researchers have become dependent on using online sources of data. However, these sources may be absent in other countries because the relevant information has not been computerized due to the cost. In this case, researchers will need to find and analyse original documents and sources, but even then, they may experience problems because the data may not be accurate. In some countries, the purpose of collecting data may not have been to provide an objective source of information for researchers. Rather, the purpose may have been to only collect data that supported government policy.

Everyone constructs stereotypes of groups of people different from themselves. These stereotypes take the qualities of a few members of a group and project them onto all members of that group. People construct stereotypes, either positive or negative, to make sense of the world.

A researcher may have a positive stereotype of groups based on perceived personality traits. However, some stereotypes held by researchers may be negative. While stereotypes can be used as a 'shorthand' method of understanding the world, the problem is that they may blind researchers to reality. If a researcher holds the stereotypes mentioned, they are much less likely to notice secondary research that contradicts these already formed views. Researchers will only notice these traits if they are very extreme because they conflict with their stereotypes.

It is impossible for researchers to be free of all stereotypes. Researchers are naturally more likely to feel positively about groups that they associate with positive personal qualities and to feel negatively about a group that they associate with negative qualities. Rather than be free of all stereotypes, the goal is for researchers to be aware of their stereotypes and to make the necessary adjustments in their attitudes.

Discussion questions

1   What is the difference between primary and secondary data?
2   Why is credibility such an important issue when conducting secondary research?
3   For what type of research questions might government data be helpful?
4   What social media sites would be useful in finding information on current consumer trends?
5   For what type of research issues is secondary data useful?
6   How can secondary data be useful in preparing primary research methods?

Answer these questions to continue creating a marketing research plan

1   What quantitative secondary data sources will be useful in answering the research question?
2   How can qualitative sources of data be useful?
3   How long will the research process take?
4   What budget will be needed?

References

Arline, Katherine. "What is Market Intelligence"? *Business News Daily*. January 29, 2019. www.businessnewsdaily.com/4697-market-intelligence.html. Accessed March 3, 2021.

Boyd, Josh. "10 Essential Marketing Research Methods." *Brand Watch*. October 24, 2019. www.brandwatch.com/blog/market-research-methods/. Accessed March 1, 2021.

Cote, Catherine. "How to Identify an Underserved Need in the Market." *Harvard Business Review*. August 11, 2020. https://online.hbs.edu/blog/post/how-to-find-a-need-in-the-market. Accessed March 31, 2021.

Fuld, Hillel. "4 Reasons Competitive Analysis is the First Step you Should Take as an Entrepreneur." *INC*. May 10, 2019. www.inc.com/hillel-fuld/4-reasons-competitive-analysis-is-first-step-y-ou-should-take-as-an-entrepreneur.html. Accessed April 12, 2021.

Hemsley, Steve. "The Rise of Automation in Market Research." *Marketing Week*. July 28, 2017. www.marketingweek.com/rise-automation-market-research/. Accessed February 26, 2021.

Shapiro, Joel. "Help Your Team Understand What Data Is and Isn't Good For." October 12, 2018. *Harvard Business Review*. https://hbr.org/2018/10/help-your-team-understand-what-data-is-and-isnt-good-for. Accessed March 8, 2021.

4 Determining the research sample

Quantitative research sampling

One of the questions researchers face when developing a research plan is who will be chosen to be research participants. The word 'population' is commonly used to define everyone of interest who could be possibly included in a research study. Researchers may define a population by geographic area. In addition, they may also define a population using such demographic data as age, gender, income, or ethnicity. Because marketing promotion is often targeted based on psychographic segmentation, researchers may also define a population based on interests, values, or lifestyles. Product usage can also be a means for defining a population, such as nonusers, occasional users, and frequent users. These variables can also be used in combination. The resulting population may be very large, such as daily drinkers of coffee who live in Berlin, or very small, such as people over the age of 70 in the city of London who are attending university as full-time students.

Sampling process

A standard process should be followed when selecting a sample. First, the population needs to be defined by demographic, psychographic, and/or geographic characteristics. The sampling frame is a list of the subjects in the sample. A method for choosing a sample from the people in the frame will be the next issue along with determining how many people need to be research subjects. Finally, the research subjects will be chosen.

Sampling process

- Decide on population to be studied.
- Develop sampling frame.
- Choose sampling method.

DOI: 10.4324/9781003165194-5

- Determine sample size.
- Choose sample participants.

Using a census

When conducting quantitative research, researchers are attempting to support a fact or hypothesis. If a 100 per cent accurate answer is needed, researchers must ask every person who is included in a population. Asking everyone in a population is called a census. Conducting a census is possible if the number of people from whom information is needed is small and all the members can be reached. If an individual wants to know how many of ten friends have purchased new shoes last month, all ten can be asked. Obviously, if the group of people being studied is large, such as the population of a city, there are problems with trying to conduct a census, so instead a sample is used.

Using a sample

Most research will involve the sampling of a population rather than a census. This is because the cost of trying to reach every possible research subject is simply too high. Less accuracy in the results will still provide the information. Even though it will result in a less accurate answer, asking a sample of the population will still provide a close enough estimate of the answer to the research question. In this type of research situation, researchers will save money and time by surveying a sample of the total population.

Target population and sampling frame

One of the most critical steps in the quantitative research process is determining the target population to be researched. It is not unusual early in the research process for both marketing researchers and the management to speak in generalities. They may discuss the need to research the attitudes of current customers who purchase frequently. They may also discuss wanting to research potential older customers. At first these might appear to be reasonable research requests. However, marketing researchers will understand that both definitions of a population are too vague. A target population always needs to be clearly defined so that the correct individuals are included in the sample frame from which the final participants will be chosen. This is especially true of the population and sampling frame for online surveys. Because geography does not need to be considered, when defining a population, it is easy to do so too broadly resulting in a higher non-response rate.

Table 4.1 Factors when determining sample size

Factor	Larger sample size needed when
Variation	More variation within a population
Precision	Small range between given and true answer
Confidence	Higher confidence that findings represent the population as a whole

Once a population has been defined, marketing researchers will be able to decide whether they can do a census of the population or whether they will need to choose a sample. If the population is small and the research question demands 100 per cent accuracy, a census could be conducted. However, in most situations, researchers will decide to use a sample of a population to participate in the survey. For a sample of participants to be chosen, researchers must first have potential access to everyone in that population.

Quantitative sampling methods

Probability sampling uses a selection method where every member of the population has an equal chance of being chosen. The methods of probability sampling from which researchers can choose include random, systematic, and stratified. These vary in the randomness of the resulting sample. They also vary in their complexity and the time and effort it will take to construct a sample.

Random sampling

The most easily understood method is simple random sampling. In this method, each sampling unit has an equal chance of being chosen to participate in the research study. The probability can be calculated by dividing the number of people in that sample by the total number of people in the population. For example, in a survey of 300 people out of a total population of 15,000, the probability of being chosen is 5 per cent, or 300 divided by 15,000.

While it is easy to calculate the probability of being chosen, what is difficult is choosing the 300 participants randomly. The problem is easy to understand if a low-tech solution to the problem is described. One way to achieve a random sample would be to write each name on a piece of paper and put all of these in a hat where there are then drawn out randomly. Of course, this would be somewhat cumbersome. Most researchers will use a random number generator. First, each name is numbered. The generator then chooses the needed number of participants at random. Students could be numbered from 1 to 15,000. Then the researcher uses the list to choose the number of the first participant. The researcher will use the next 299 numbers in the random list to determine who is included in the sample.

Systematic sampling

Even though it is a much simpler method to use, systematic sampling will result in a sample that is almost random. In systematic sampling, after the population has been determined, all units in the population are listed and counted. A skip interval is then calculated by dividing the total population by the sample size, and this interval is used to choose who will be included in the sample. Using the example described earlier, the skip interval is 50, or 15,000 divided by 300. A random start point is chosen and then the skip interval is used to count off every fiftieth name on the list which is then included in the sample. At first glance this may seem to be as random as simple sampling, but this is not so. If the list is an alphabetical listing of family names, the starting letter of family names is not random but often determined by ethnic and national origin.

One solution to this problem is to randomize the list before using the skip interval. If the list is computerized, it can be sorted by a more random factor, than name or student number. Another method is restarting the skip interval and counting once or twice when choosing the sample. Each time this happens a new random start would be chosen.

Stratified sampling

Stratified sampling is used when researchers believe that answers will vary depending on the demographic, psychographic, geographic, or usage characteristics of each person in a population. There are two main reasons for choosing a stratified sample. First, the population may be skewed in such a way that it is difficult to obtain a random sample using either a random or systematic method. In this case, stratified sampling is used to increase the randomness of the sample. Secondly, the research study may call for comparing results between specific groups within a population. The main reason for using stratified sampling is to ensure that any differences are diminished by the sampling procedure. Another reason is when the research study is designed to learn more about differences between groups.

Most populations can be divided into smaller groups based on shared characteristics. These characteristics can be based on demographic factors such as gender, age, income, and education level. They can also be grouped by psychographic characteristics such as interests and lifestyles. Geographic grouping may be an important option to consider if the answer to a research question might vary depending on where participants live. Finally, product usage status, such as nonusers, occasional users, and frequent users, might be of interest to researchers.

Using a stratified sample allows marketing researchers to examine each of the strata separately. Initially, researchers must decide how many participants will be chosen from the population. The researchers must then decide on how to distribute the number of total participants among the different strata.

Calculating sample size

Once a sampling procedure has been chosen, researchers must then decide upon the number of subjects that should be included in the research to ensure that the results are representative of the entire population. Research costs money, and the more research subjects that are involved, the more the study will cost. If carefully chosen, a small sample from this population can be reasonably representative of the whole.

There are a few concepts that must be considered when sample size is determined. First, the more variation there is in a population, the larger a sample will need to be. A second factor that must be considered in this example is the precision in the range between the survey answer results and the reality of the population. A third factor that must be considered when determining sample size is the need for confidence that the research findings reflect the reality of the total population. Total accuracy requires a census of all participants. Since this is not possible, the organization must decide what level of confidence they need that the survey data accurately reflect the whole. The larger a sample is compared to the total population, the higher will be the confidence that this is so. However, this does not mean that a larger sample is always better (Devault 2020). Once a sample gets to be in the range of 1,500 participants, adding more people to the study does not increase the confidence level enough to justify the cost.

To calculate the necessary size of a sample, it is not necessary to know the size of the population. What is needed are the variation in the population, the acceptable range of the estimated answer from the true answer, and the confidence level that the calculated answer is correct. While the basic formula for calculating the sample when estimating an average or mean is quite simple, there are online sites that will provide sample size calculators. The calculator will ask for the confidence level that is needed that the answer is accurate for the population. The usual confidence level used is 95 per cent confidence that the answer from the sample will be correct for the population. The margin of error that will need to be input is a percentage measure of the variability of the answers. Using these three numbers, the required sample size can be calculated.

Qualitative research sampling

The choice of subjects for qualitative research involves non-random sampling. When using non-random sampling, everyone in the population does not have an equal chance to be chosen as part of the sample. However, non-random does not mean that a marketing researcher chooses the participants haphazardly or without thought. Even when conducting non-random sampling for focus groups, interviews, and observational research, subjects will still need to be chosen carefully. There are three basic issues to be considered for selecting research participants which include demographic and psychographic characteristics, a knowledge of the research issue, and the geographical location where potential participants live.

The description of which characteristics need to be considered when choosing research subjects is called the participant profile. While there are similarities in the process for choosing participants for each type of qualitative research methodology, there are also specific issues related to the selection process that differ.

Recruitment of individuals for participation in focus groups requires the selection of subjects with specific demographic and psychographic characteristics from within a population. Researchers may decide that the sample to include in the research study will be based on demographics such as age, gender, income, or ethnicity. These characteristics may be the most important considerations when choosing a sample because the research involves examining the purchasing behaviour of one of these specific consumer segments. In addition, a new product may be targeted at a specific psychographic group based on their lifestyle or interests. Therefore, it is imperative that researchers include those participants who share these psychographic characteristics so that companies can learn more about their wants and needs.

For some qualitative techniques, particularly those that require significant participant interaction, another step may be added to the process. If participants will be required to work extensively with projective techniques, researchers will want to know if they will be sufficiently motivated to give their full attention and creativity to the process. In this instance, researchers may want to hold a short pre-focus group where they can get to know the personalities of potential participants. Only those whom the researchers feel will add to the dynamics of the focus group would be invited to participate (Boedeker 2021). Because fewer participants are involved, it is essential that only the appropriate individuals are asked.

Selection issues for focus groups

The location where focus group potential participants live is also a consideration when choosing the sample, as they must be willing to travel to the location where the focus group is being held. If participants do not live within a short traveling distance, they may not be willing to travel to take part. This is one reason for using online focus groups so that distance is not an issue. Least in importance is that participants have a particular knowledge about the specific research issues. Focus group participants may be selected by usage level, but they will not be expected to have any specific knowledge of the relevant industry or of its competitors.

Selection issues for interviews

Researchers recruiting a sample for interviews will need to find fewer participants. However, because there are usually only a few interviews conducted, it is important to choose each participant carefully. To do so researchers will develop a participant profile based on knowledge of the research issue with personal characteristics being a secondary consideration. This makes selection more difficult as potential interview subjects must be screened about their knowledge level. However, fewer participants are needed because of the time it takes to conduct the interviews. Personal characteristics must also be considered to ensure that the views expressed will provide insight into the target market segment of interest to the company involved.

Location is less important when considering the choice of participants. The knowledge the potential participants have is valuable, but it is not reasonable to assume that potential research subjects will be willing to travel to meet with researchers. Instead, researchers will have to travel to interview these experts or the company concerned must be willing to pay for the research participants' travel expenses. The challenge in finding participants will be the time that it takes to choose the correct participants when arranging the interview. It is fortunate that technology can allow direct online communication without travel.

Selection issues for observation research

Observation also involves choosing participants. However, with observation the location is the most important choice criterion. Observational research will always take place where participants are involved in the behaviour under study. Therefore, it is this choice of location that is the most important decision when choosing a sample. If the wrong location is chosen, it will be impossible to observe the right participants.

Of course, the choice of location is also based on the personal characteristics of the desired research subjects who will be found there. Because not everyone at the location is of interest to the researchers, they will have to choose potential subjects based on their personal characteristics. For observational research, these characteristics must be discernible through observation. Even then researchers will need to make a judgment call, personal characteristics such as age would be described in general categories such as 'young aged, 18–22' or 'middle aged, 40–55'. When conducting observational research, researchers gain data without verbal communication as it is behaviour, and not knowledge, that is studied. Here technology has also assisted researchers. A video tape can be analysed, or cameras and computers can watch subjects even when the researchers are located elsewhere.

Professional recruiters

It can take considerable time and effort to find qualified research subjects for qualitative research. Some researchers may also feel they do not have the expertise to find appropriate subjects. This is especially true if the research subjects are from a population that is ethnically or culturally different from that of the researchers. Professional research subject recruiting firms can provide assistance in these situations. These companies continually recruit subjects who are promised payment for their participation. The subjects a research company may need could already be in an existing database compiled by a professional recruiter. Alternatively, they can recruit participants who will be needed for studying a unique segment.

Qualitative sampling methods

There are three basic methods for constructing a qualitative participant sample. Researchers can use convenience sampling, where they ask any individuals who are willing to participate. Snowballing is a system where an appropriate potential participant is identified and is then asked to recruit others with similar characteristics. When using purposive sampling, researchers select potential participants that best meet the sample profile. For all three of these methods, the question remains how many people should be

Table 4.2 Methods of sample selection for qualitative research

Method	Steps
Convenience	Find the correct population Choose those most likely to participate
Snowballing	Choose first participant in population based on profile Ask chosen participant to identify others Verify that the referrals meet the profile Invite referrals to participate
Purposive	Identify the characteristics Develop a list of potential participants Invite them to participate

involved in the qualitative research. There is no rule or formula for the correct number. One concept that can help is saturation. If the researchers are not uncovering any new ideas or concepts, they have probably involved enough participants for the research to be considered valid.

Convenience and snowballing sampling

Convenience sampling is used when researchers choose any willing and available individuals that match the profile as participants. This method can be implemented when it is known that a specific location tends to attract the type of individual needed for that research study. The recruitment of participants can then take place in this location as it is where people who meet the profile tend to congregate.

Another method of choosing participants is called 'snowball' sampling. With this method researchers choose the first participant to match the participant profile. This participant then refers others with similar characteristics. The theory for using this system is that the first participant is more likely to know someone like themselves than the researchers. This method is appropriate when the research calls for participants who may be from psychographic or ethnic groups that are very different from those of the researchers. There are two reasons for using snowballing. First, researchers may not have a knowledge of the relevant participants. Secondly, even if they did, potential participants may not respond to an invitation from the researchers to participate. This may be because they do not understand the process or trust the researchers.

When using the snowball process, researchers should choose the first participant carefully. The success of any research will depend on their accurate referral of similar participants. Once additional participants are referred, it should still be verified that they meet the stated requirements. These participants will then recruit others and so on until enough participants have been found. Technology can now be used to track the invitations and responses, which simplifies the process (Sun 2017).

When this has happened, participants are then sent information on the research study and an invitation to take part. Even when a non-probability sampling method such as snowballing is used, the final group of participants should always be analysed to see if they are substantially different from the profile.

Purposive sampling

The research question will define the characteristics of the participant profile. It is important that the participants chosen to match this profile have the necessary common experiences which will result in useful research data. If input is needed from more than one type of research subject, then more than one participant profile should be developed, and two groups of potential subjects will need to be recruited.

The process of using purposive sampling first includes establishing the participant profile. Then a list of potential research subjects is identified that have the needed characteristics and knowledge. Finally, specific individuals from this list are asked to participate. Researchers may sometimes need to find participants for more than one type of methodology: it is not uncommon for large companies to conduct more than one type of qualitative research at a time.

Qualitative research is only effective if the right participants are selected. Purposive sampling is the best method to ensure that this occurs. Researchers will have spent considerable time and effort on the design of a research methodology, but the best methodology will fail if the wrong participants are chosen to participate. The purposive sampling process first involves identifying key characteristics of the individuals who should participate. These will include their demographic characteristics, such as age, gender, income, and education level. Psychographic characteristics such as lifestyle, attitudes, opinions, and values may also be relevant. The geographic area within which participants should live is important. The product knowledge or usage pattern of the participants is relevant if the research question distinguishes between non-users, occasional users, and heavy product users. Once these characteristics are determined, management and researchers will determine the organizations or groups where individuals with these characteristics can be found. Specific individuals from these groups are then invited to participate in the research study.

A participant profile with very specific and detailed characteristics makes recruitment even more challenging. In this case it may be necessary to place advertisements on social media to find the right people (James 2021). The ad should state the requirements, the purpose of the study, and any incentive that is being offered. The market researchers must then verify that each of the selected participants does meet the requirements. The ads should be on the social media sites that are most likely to be used by members of the targeted groups.

Identifying organizations or groups

After the characteristics that define the desired participants are selected, the next step in the process is to identify the groups with which these potential participants might associate. It may be that the researchers or management know people who fit the profile, but this would be the exception rather than the rule. Even if the researchers do know appropriate potential subjects, these are not the persons who should be selected. If the potential participants have an existing relationship with a researcher, they may not give objective answers.

If a participant profile calls for current product users, they may be found using internal company information, such as mailing lists or customer databases. For a small business, participants who are product users may be chosen from frequent customers who are currently known to the owner. A participant profile may call for people who are nonusers. One way to locate these potential participants is by using organizational memberships. An effective means of finding participants is to choose an organization that has members who are similar to those who meet the profile of potential participants. Such an organization may be a business membership group, social or service club, civic organization, non-profit group, church, or sports team. If the organization has members that meet the profile, an incentive to participate may be offered. However, all researchers should be aware that offering incentives can alter the type of people who agree to participate (Wolff-Eisenberg 2016).

Participants can also be found by posting an invitation to participate on websites or social media sites. This method is used when potential participants may not be members of any official organization. They can post a request on a web or social media site that is of interest to the targeted group. The researchers may need to provide an incentive of specific interest to the targeted group to encourage participation. This incentive should be communicated in the research participant's request.

Once a list of potential participants has been created, a few short screening questions should be prepared. These questions will verify if the potential research subjects meet the profile determined by the researchers. The questions can be administered orally, and the answers recorded, or a potential participant can be asked to complete the questionnaire.

Discussion questions

1   What would be the advantages of using a sample versus conducting a census for a consumer behaviour study?
2   What nonprobability sampling methods are available when choosing participants for surveys?
3   What sample selection methods are available when choosing participants for focus groups?
4   Why are personal characteristics more important criteria for focus group participants for surveys?
5   How could the use of incentives to recruit participants bias the outcome of a study?

6   In what type of situation would it be more appropriate to use a professional recruiter to find research subjects?
7   Why could it be argued that psychographic characteristics are more important to consider than demographic characteristics when conducting qualitative research?

Answer these questions to continue to create a marketing research plan

1   How can the population to be studied be defined?
2   How will the sample of participants be chosen?
3   Where can the potential participants be found?
4   How will participants be invited to participate?

References

Boedeker, Gina. "Top Pitfalls in Planning and Executing Effective Focus Groups." *Forbes*, February 1, 2021. www.forbes.com/sites/forbesbusiness-council/2021/02/01/top-pitfalls-in-planning-and-executing-effective-focus-groups/?sh=32fdcb325116. Accessed March 8, 2021.

Devault, Gigi. "Avoid these Bias Errors in Social Media Research." *The Balance Small Business*. January 13, 2020. www.thebalancesmb.com/avoid-bias-errors-in-social-media-research-2297091. Accessed March 10, 2021.

James, Greg. "Research Recruiting: How to use Marketing Strategies to Find Participants." *User Interviews*. February 11, 2021. www.userinterviews.com/blog/research-recruiting-on-facebook-and-other-strategies. Accessed March 29, 2021.

Sun, Jenny. "How to Find, Screen and Schedule Participants for User Research." *Field UX*. October 1, 2017. www.fieldux.com/how-to-find-screen-and-schedule-participants-for-user-research/. Accessed February 19, 2021.

Wolff-Eisenberg, Christine. 2016. "Survey Administration Best Practices: Using Incentives Effectively." ITHAKA S+R. January 27, 2016. www.sr.ithaka.org/blog/survey-administration-best-practices-using-incentives-effectively/. Accessed January 28, 2021.

5   Writing quantitative research surveys

Survey questionnaire design and testing

Survey is a quantitative research methodology that consists of a set of questions with predetermined answers from which participants must choose. In addition, some survey questions may be open-ended, where participants are able to respond in their own words. Surveys can be administered by a researcher, either in person, with a video link, or over the phone. Surveys can also be self-administered whereby they are sent via the postal service, sent by email, or posted on social media. Whatever the form of survey administration, the survey design methodology and the questionnaire development process remain basically the same.

Surveys are most effective when obtaining information if marketing researchers already know something about the research problem being studied. This information will be needed as researchers must anticipate participants' responses when they write possible answers to questions. Such knowledge can be the result of secondary research on the external environment or already conducted qualitative research. Surveys can be used to gather information on any aspect of the marketing mix, including the customer, product, promotion, price, and distribution.

Questionnaire development needs

When designing a questionnaire for a survey, a researcher must keep in mind the needs of several groups, that may have an interest in what questions will be on the survey form. Each group will view the completed questionnaire from their own unique perspective. First, the management of the company that has commissioned the research will be concerned that the survey questions will provide the information needed to answer the research question. In addition, they will also want questions on demographic and geographic characteristics that will allow for comparisons and contrasts between groups of consumers.

DOI: 10.4324/9781003165194-6

Table 5.1 Purpose of survey research

Marketing mix element	Possible research issues
Customer	Satisfaction of current segment towards product
	Find new customer segment to target with product
Product	Preferred benefits of current product
	Benefits desired from new product
Promotion	Awareness of promotional campaign components
	Effectiveness of promotional campaign to motivate purchase
Price	Appropriate pricing level
	Effect of price increase on purchase behaviour
Place	Location where product should be sold
	Ease of purchase process

The research participants will want the questions to be ones they can answer and that are worded in a way that is easily understood. Participants will also want the form designed so that it is simple to record their responses. Those administering the survey (if it is not self-administered) will want the questions to be written clearly so that participants do not need to ask for clarification.

Once management has determined the research question, the questionnaire design process will begin with a meeting between researchers and management. At this meeting, researchers and management will discuss the topic areas that need to be covered in the survey to provide the data needed to answer all aspects of the research question. An issue that arises when writing survey question is a belief on the part of management as to the source of the problem (Herzog, Hattula and Dahl 2021). This can influence the decision as to what survey questions should be asked. For this reason, researchers should only write the draft survey after initial secondary research. This draft will then be reviewed by management for the appropriateness of the questions.

Another issue that needs to be addressed is how the process needs to be adapted if the survey study is to be conducted in a different country or with participants from a different cultural group. This process will be repeated until everyone is satisfied with both the questions and the answers. The questionnaire will then be laid out in its final form. The last step will be to test the survey with potential participants.

Writing the draft and management review

Once the sample questions have been approved, a draft survey needs to be created. Researchers will then review the form with the management of the company to determine the appropriateness of the questions and to check if any additional questions should be asked. This process might be repeated any number of times. While it is management's responsibility to decide on the topic areas, each time the form is reviewed it is the marketing researchers' responsibility to explain why certain questions should be included and why some should not be asked. The exact wording of the questions also needs to be reviewed. This process must be repeated until everyone is comfortable with the survey questions. Trying to save time at this step in the process may result in wrong or badly worded questions being asked, with the result being unusable data. In addition, at this stage in the process, the answers to the questions must also be developed. Other issues that will need to be discussed will include translation issues that must be addressed even for single-country surveys. In addition, the organization and design of the physical layout of the form need to be discussed.

In the past it was not uncommon for a marketing survey project to take six to eight weeks to complete. With the fast pace of global change this has become too long for many organizations (Larson 2020). Using communication technology can speed the process while still going through all the steps. If the survey process takes too long, the results may no longer be applicable to the problem.

Testing the survey form

All survey forms should be tested. When testing the survey form, both the content of questions and their wording should be examined. Each question should be one that the participant can and is willing to answer. In addition, the wording should be checked to see if a participant understands the question in the way that the researchers intended. Besides the questions, the answers should also be examined. The available responses for a question should contain the answers that most participants would provide. If the written answer does not do so, 'other' will be ticked too often, or participants will choose a response even though it does not accurately reflect their opinions.

In addition to the content and wording, the form of each question should be examined. If an open-ended question leaves a participant confused, it can be rewritten as a close-ended question with potential answers provided. The words used in the scale that is used to answer a question, such as 'strongly agree' to 'strongly disagree', should have the same meaning for all participants. Lastly, the instructions should be tested to ensure that they are written in an easily understandable format.

The survey questionnaire should be tested to ensure that the results will be useable (Fisher 2020). The testing should be conducted with participants who are like the research subject sample. If the sample consists of a variety of subgroups, at least some of the test participants should be from each group. During

Table 5.2 Survey process

Steps for all surveys
Write research question
Select sample
Decide upon method of surveying
Write and test survey
Select times and/or locations to conduct survey

Steps for researcher administered survey	Steps for self-administered survey
Identify needed staffing	Leave for pickup, mail or open website
Hire and train survey takers	Wait for results
Conduct survey	Analyse and report findings
Analyse and report findings	

the first step in the testing process, a researcher should be present while a participant completes the questionnaire. This way the researcher can make a note of any direction, question, or answer that causes difficulty. If there are major problems with the survey form, the researcher should address these through changes and the testing should begin again. If there are only a few minor changes that result from testing the questionnaire, the testing can proceed to the next step.

Writing the questions

Most survey questions are close ended, with possible answers provided from which a participant must choose. These answers can be based on previous qualitative research, such as focus groups or interviews. For example, the answers that focus group participants provide most frequently to a similar question will determine the responses used on the survey form. In addition, data discovered through observation and interviews will also be used to construct the answers to close-ended questions.

Open-ended questions allow survey participants to provide their own answers that they will write on the form or type online. Since the purpose of surveys, which are a quantitative research methodology, is to support a fact or hypothesis, open-ended questions must be kept to a minimum. This is because the answers to open-ended questions may vary so much that there aren't enough similar responses to allow for statistical calculations.

General guidelines for question writing

There are general guidelines that researchers should remember when writing any survey question. First, the questions should not be hypothetical, as some people will have difficulty imagining such situations. For example, questions that ask for imaged responses such as 'How would you feel if you found out that you had bought defective merchandise?' are difficult to answer on a survey form. Such questions are best left to focus groups or interviews where researchers have the time to draw out responses. Survey questions should only deal with what participants already know.

Researchers are often very familiar with the terminology used by the industry commissioning the research. If not initially, they will have certainly become familiar with the industry terminology while conducting secondary research. It is important for researchers to remember that participants in a survey might not have this knowledge. Researchers should always write the question using words that are commonly understood.

Besides the issue of terminology, respondents may not read at the same academic level as researchers. Reading level involves the number of words in a sentence, the sentence's grammatical structure, and the length of the words used. It is very important to have questions written at the correct level. If researchers are unsure they should always write at a lower level, which will make a sentence easier and quicker to read for everyone.

It is important to keep a survey form short so that participants are motivated to complete it. However, researchers should not be tempted to shorten the number of questions by combining more than one at a time. Asking two questions simultaneously will only confuse participants. If a participant is unsure of the question being asked, the answer will be meaningless.

Questions that ask if 'a person' or 'someone' has done something will leave respondents confused. They will find it easiest to respond to questions that ask about their own activities. For example, a question such as 'Do people buy products that they have seen on infomercials?' cannot be answered as participants will not have such knowledge. A question that asks, 'Do you purchase products that you have seen on infomercials?' is easy to understand.

The translation may be necessary even when a questionnaire is being used in only one country. Even simple words such as 'miserable', 'disgusted', or 'thrilled' will be difficult to translate with the exact same level of meaning.

Writing the answers

There are two components to a survey answer. These are the wording of the answer and the means of response. The same rules that apply to writing the questions apply to writing the answers, but even more so. Because each answer consists of so few words, it is vitally important that these are the right words. There are several ways that participants can be instructed to answer a question. An answer to the question of 'What motivated you to enrol in this marketing course?' could be written using fill-in-the-blank, dichotomous, forced choice, multiple choice, checklist, rating, and ranking responses.

Open-ended questions, where respondents are only provided with a blank line, are used when researchers do not wish to lead participants. An example of an open-ended question in a survey would be 'Why did you enrol in this marketing course?' The advantage of this type of question is that it allows any type of response, including those which researchers might not have thought of. One surprising response might be 'A person I'm attracted to signed up'. After all, potential romance might not have been among the responses considered by researchers. The disadvantage of this type of fill-in-the-blank response is that every questionnaire will have to be read and the answer will need to be analysed.

A dichotomous choice answer allows respondents to choose one of two responses that are usually opposite. Examples would be answers that allow respondents to tick 'yes' or 'no'. A dichotomous choice answer directly addresses a research issue and forces participants to make a choice. Perhaps researchers are interested in discovering whether the love of learning motivates students to enrol in a marketing course. However, this response may not be one that occurs to a student. This would leave researchers with the conclusion that love of learning plays no role in motivations for enrolling in the class. A dichotomous choice question would ask, 'Is love of learning one of the reasons why you enrolled in this course?' The student will tick either 'yes' or 'no'. This type of answer forces students to reveal whether the love of learning had any role in motivating their decision.

A forced choice question asks respondents to choose between two responses. However, the responses do not need to be opposites. In fact, they can have no direct relationship with each other. Researchers would use this type of question when they want to determine which of the two responses is more important. It might be that researchers notice that mid-afternoon classes have the most enrolments. Is this because of a popular professor or the time of day? In this case the forced choice answers would be written as 'Like to take mid-afternoon classes so I can work later' and 'Heard the professor was friendly'. Therefore, a student cannot choose both. If most of the students tick the first answer, mid-afternoon might be the time to schedule professors who have lower enrolments because students do not perceive them as friendly!

When researchers have a number of variables that might affect choice, they may wish to write a multiple-choice question. The answers would then list the motivations that were uncovered during earlier exploratory research. Researchers must decide how many reasons to list. If too many are provided, participants may find it difficult to weigh them mentally and conclude which are most important. It is common to list four or five possible answers. Of course, the listed reasons might not include any of the reasons why an individual student might have enrolled in that class. This situation can be handled by adding 'none of the above' as a response or by allowing a fill-in-the-blank line for respondents to write in their own responses.

The problem with a multiple-choice answer is that more than one of the answers may be true. A student might have been strongly motivated by two or even three of the reasons. A checklist solves this problem by allowing participants to choose as many variables as possible. Because participants do not have to weigh one possible answer against another, a checklist can include many more possible answers.

A variation on the checklist is the ranking question. This type of question and answer assumes that the listed responses will include several variables that will apply. It allows participants to indicate not only which of the reasons apply but also the relative importance of each reason. Theoretically, researchers could ask participants to rank all the answers that apply. However, this may prove to be too difficult for participants, so usually a question will ask participants to rank their top three to five answers.

The importance of asking a ranking question instead of just providing a checklist will become apparent when data analysis is considered. In data analysis, when calculating the frequency of responses, they will not just be counted but will also be weighted by choice. For example, the number one choice for students might vary widely, while the second choice is almost always 'It will help me get a job'. When the variables are weighted, the choice that was second ranked may be the most common.

A rating question will allow respondents to choose more than one answer and also to rank the importance of each. The answer can consist of three, five, or seven possible rankings. One of the rankings will be that the answer had no effect on choice. This is always the middle of the rating. A researcher can then write the rating to allow a respondent to indicate whether the answer had either a positive or negative effect on choice, such as 'agree' or 'disagree'.

In addition, the ratings can allow participants to show how strongly the answer positively or negatively affected their choice. Even complex questions can be answered in this way. A researcher may obtain this information by adding more possible answers, such as 'strongly agree' and 'strongly disagree'. Along with the response of 'no effect', the answer now has five possibilities. A researcher can continue to expand the answer to add the responses of 'very strongly agree' and 'very strongly disagree'. Of course, it is still difficult to predict how each participant will evaluate the choice of rating.

Questionnaire layout

For self-administered surveys, the way that the questions and answers are visually presented is critical. This is true for both paper and online survey forms. A poorly laid-out questionnaire may confuse participants and result in unanswered questions. When laying out a form, researchers must remember the visual impact that results from the use of margins, spacing, and font size. Proper use of these elements will result in a survey form that is visually appealing and easy for the participants to read.

Researchers will also want to keep a survey form to as few pages as possible, as fewer pages will keep reproduction costs down. Whether on paper or online, a survey with many pages will discourage potential subjects from participating. However, these concerns should not lead researchers to print the survey in a font that is too small and therefore difficult to read. The use of white space, such as larger margins and extra lines between the questions, will result in a longer survey form but will also make the survey more attractive.

Routing is an issue that needs to be considered when a questionnaire layout is designed. For example, there might be a follow-up question designed only for those who drive an automobile to go shopping. A question that asks where participants park their car when they travel to the store will not be relevant for those participants who took the bus. Therefore, these participants should be directed to skip the question and go on to the next question. The instructions for routing must be very clearly and simply stated on the survey form as most people will assume that they will need to answer every question. One advantage of an online survey is that it can be programmed to automatically bring the subject to the next appropriate question.

Question sequence

The questions should not be listed on the form in a random manner. The initial questions should be for the purpose of qualifying a participant. The types of qualification questions asked would depend on the research question and the purpose of the survey. They may ask a participant about the frequency of purchase of a specific consumer product or whether they rent or own their own home. The questions may also ask about age or family status.

Even if basic demographic data are not part of the qualifications or research question, they should still be included. These demographic questions should come first as they are the easiest to answer. For example, while the research question might not have asked about a gender difference in purchase habits or attitudes, when the data are analysed, it may be found that there is a difference in consumption based on age, education level, and even geographic location. However, there is now sensitivity on how the demographic question on gender is asked. As many social groups have urged going beyond the simple male-versus-female choice, the question of gender becomes complicated (Gossett 2020). The issue of whether a service or product should be only considered appropriate for a single gender also arises. The researchers may decide to not include any questions on gender for these reasons.

The next questions should be general in nature, with more in-depth questions to follow. For example, a question that asks what brand of sneakers a participant prefers is easy to answer. A more specific question, as to why the participant chooses to purchase this specific brand with many possible answers, will take more thought. If difficult questions are listed on a survey form too early on, they may discourage participants from continuing and completing the form. Also for this reason, any sensitive questions, such as "Do you feel when you have to buy a larger clothing size?" should be saved for last.

Question sequence

- Qualifying questions.
- Demographic questions.
- Easy-to-answer questions.
- In-depth questions.
- Sensitive questions.

Online survey forms

The development of an online survey should be no different from that of a traditional survey. There are software packages now available that make the creation of a survey much easier. However, this does not make the decision of what topics to address and how to write the questions and potential answers any easier. While some programs provide pre-written questions on a variety of subjects, the researcher should be careful to ensure the questions used are specific to the current research project. With the popularity of people searching for information on their phones, the survey must also be able to be seen easily on a cell phone screen. Short survey forms may be developed that can even be texted to participants (Marlar 2017).

There are several reasons for the increasing popularity of putting survey forms online. One is the difficulty in motivating individuals to participate in traditional survey research. An online form can be completed at a time that is convenient for a participant, unlike a phone or personal survey. Also, the completed form is automatically returned – unlike a mail survey.

In addition, there are design advantages to using an electronic form. With an electronic form, there is less concern to keep a questionnaire to as few pages as possible. Participants only see one or two questions at a time and, therefore, will not be intimidated by the overall length. In addition, the form can be laid with colourful graphics that make it visually appealing.

The form can be designed so that the next question that needs to be answered will appear on the screen based on the answer to the previous question. On an electronic survey form, when a participant responds to a question on how they travel to the store with the answer 'by car', the next question will automatically ask about the difficulty of parking. If the response to the question is not 'by bus', the next question will ask about the convenience of the bus stop.

Another advantage to laying out an electronic survey form is the ability to use drop-down boxes for answers to questions. In written surveys, researchers face the temptation of limiting the number of responses provided to any one question so that the survey form does not become too lengthy. Using drop-down boxes that allow participants to use their cursors to see a list of answers and then make their choice solves this problem. The answers can then be listed in random order for each survey form. This helps to eliminate the bias of clicking on the first answer provided.

Administering the survey

A researcher or an assistant can administer survey forms, or these can be self-administered. The methods for administered surveys include in person, computer-aided personal surveying, and by telephone. The advantages of these methods include the ability to clarify misunderstandings, to prompt completion, and to establish rapport. Self-administered surveying includes mail, web-based forms, and, for very short surveys, texting. The advantages to self-administered surveys include less cost, an inability for researchers to bias the response, and participants' ability to complete at their own pace and convenience.

Personal surveying has the advantage of allowing the use of visual prompts. A researcher can also demonstrate product use. Computer-aided personal surveys use a hand-held device to collect answers. This reduces the cost of data entry while also making complex question sequencing easy to understand. Telephone surveys suffer from low response rates, but they still have the advantage of reaching certain groups and providing anonymity.

Email surveys are inexpensive, and with this methodology, there is no danger of an interviewer biasing the response. The success of email surveys depends on the quality of the email list used to reach participants. Online surveys can be easy to create and provide researchers with the ability to see results immediately and to track response rates. In addition, results can be analysed immediately. The disadvantage is that a sample may be skewed towards younger and professional people.

To motivate completion, information that is provided to participants should explain the reason for the research and why a certain subject has been chosen. It should also assure confidentiality and provide contact information for those who wish to assure themselves regarding the legitimacy of the research. Information should also be provided on any financial or product incentive that will be given to the research subject.

The survey process starts with writing the research question, selecting the sample, and the method of surveying. If the survey is to be administered, the process must include the training of survey takers. Survey takers should train by practicing giving the survey to each other. The trainers should monitor the first surveys conducted by the survey takers.

Discussion questions

1   Why is testing of a survey form important?
2   Why does an online survey form need to go through the same development process?
3   What are the advantages of having researchers personally conduct surveys?
4   Why is it becoming more difficult to get people to respond to any survey?
5   What information would be important to include in a covering email or social media post when conducting an online survey?
6   Why would it be critical to train survey takers who were going to conduct a survey of minority populations?

Answer these questions to continue creating a marketing research plan

1   What survey questions will be asked?
2   What type of answers should be allowed?
3   How will the survey be distributed?
4   How will participants be incentivized to participate?

References

Fisher, Sarah. "7 Ways to Pretest Your Survey Before You Send it." *Qualtrics.* November 13, 2020. Available from www.qualtrics.com/blog/6-ways-to-pretest-your-survey-before-you-send-it/. Accessed January 22, 2021.

Gossett, Stephen. "Dscout Discusses How to Collect User Data on Gender Identity – and When Not To." *Builtin.* September 2, 2020. https://builtin.com/data-science/dscout-gender-identity-data-practice. January 31, 2021.

Herzog, Walter, Johannes D. Hattual and Darren W. Dahl. "Marketers Project Their Personal Preferences onto Consumers: Overcoming the Threat of Egocentric Decision Making." *Journal of Marketing Research*. February 10, 2021. Accessed March 1, 2021.

Larson, Jill. "A New Beginning for Marketing Research." *Forbes*. December 21, 2020. www.forbes.com/sites/sap/2020/12/21/a-new-beginning-for-market-research/ ?sh=31bff01b36a5. Accessed April 1, 2021.

Marlar, Jenny. "Using Text Messaging to Reach Survey Respondents." *Gallup*. November 11, 2017. https://news.gallup.com/opinion/methodology/221159/using-text-messaging-reach-survey-respondents.aspx. Accessed March 13, 2021.

6 Conducting qualitative focus groups

Focus group methodology

A marketing research focus group is a methodology that uses participant interaction and moderator probing to uncover consumer wants, needs, and desires. A focus group is sometimes misunderstood as being a mere discussion group, where a moderator introduces a topic and then sits back and takes notes. However, it is the interaction between the moderator and group members and also between the members themselves that gets beyond participants' first responses to explore deeper motivations.

The focus group is designed to collect data and not just to air opinions. This interaction distinguishes focus groups from other types of group sessions, such as group interviews that do not encourage interaction between research participants. Used correctly, focus groups are an excellent method of generating new ideas for product benefits and promotions, exploring the causes for problems or failures, and gaining insights that can then be used to design quantitative research studies.

Focus groups are probably most frequently used as a means of generating new ideas. Product development is ultimately the responsibility of company employees. Although these employees may have marketing expertise, it is customers who will make the purchase decision. It only makes sense to ask customers for assistance in generating ideas for new or improved products. In addition, focus groups can be used to generate ideas on new promotional campaigns, including effective marketing messages and appropriate choices of media.

Focus groups are also used to learn the 'why' or cause of problems or failures. The problems explored in a focus group could be why a product is not succeeding in the marketplace. It may seem to be a simple task to ask consumers why they don't like a product. For example, a simple question such as why consumers do not purchase a food product might receive the response that consumers do not like the taste. The problem is that simply

DOI: 10.4324/9781003165194-7

telling the marketing department to improve the taste of a product does not provide any information on what consumers did not like and what they would like instead. In the case of a service product, consumers might say that staff were rude. However, without any information on why consumers felt staff were rude, there is nothing for management to use in order to improve. Focus groups will explore the reasons for these problems in depth, thus providing ideas a company can use to solve the problem.

Focus groups are often conducted to generate a hypothesis that will be used in future quantitative research (Stromberg 2019). For example, they can be used to gain insights that would help a researcher to write future survey questions. While the survey questions about why a product is liked or disliked are easy to write, the answers are not. This is because there are so many potential answers as preferences vary widely. Focus groups can be used to gather information on the answers that should be included in a survey. For example, focus groups may have provided information that consumers are concerned about a specific product's colour, size, and shape, and this information can then be included on the subsequent survey form.

Rationale for using focus groups

An advantage of using focus groups is the opportunity they provide for researchers to probe issues in depth by encouraging interaction between members. In addition, if a moderator is unsure of any point made by participants, they can be asked follow-up questions. Finally, a focus group can be combined with the use of projective techniques to elicit nonverbal responses.

The major advantage to using a focus group is the interaction that encourages spontaneity. In a one-on-one interview, a participant might place a researcher in a position of authority. As a result, this participant may not want to disagree or express negative opinions. In a focus group, participants will not feel that they must agree with the opinions of other participants. As a result, they will be much more likely to disagree and express their own ideas. In addition, unlike an interview, participants do not need to speak until they feel that they have something they want to say. As a result, individuals will find a focus group a much less intimidating experience than an individual interview.

One of the advantages of a focus group over a survey is the ability of the moderator to ask follow-up questions. When a participant responds to a question with a general comment that they do not 'like' a product, the moderator can keep asking for additional information. The final answer may be that the participant does not like the colour, size, taste, packaging, or cost. The moderator can then ask what they might prefer.

Combine with other research methods

While focus groups allow participants to interact with each other and the moderator, they also allow participants to interact with their physical surroundings. To help gain information, a moderator may allow the participants to handle or taste the physical product. This method could not be used when conducting a survey. In addition, the focus group methodology can be combined with projective techniques by using video clips of the product in action.

In the past, marketing research was often viewed as an either/or proposition. Either researchers believed in the primacy of quantitative research or they were believers in qualitative research. Even if researchers prefer using quantitative research, they should consider combining methodologies. Once ideas, such as new brand names, promotional messages, and product benefits, are generated by a focus group, they can then be further researched using a quantitative technique such as a survey. This type of two-stage research project uses the advantages of both qualitative and quantitative research by first generating ideas and then confirming them. While taking more time and resources than a single study, such a two-stage study makes sense when expensive decisions must be made. This is because the cost to a company of a wrong decision can be very high.

Focus group process

The focus group method consists of the three stages of preparing, conducting, and analysing. Preparation for a focus group requires that researchers meet with management to discuss the research objectives. The researchers together with management will then develop the research participant profile, after which the participants will be invited and a moderator will be chosen. The researchers will then use both the research objectives and the participant profile to write a focus group script. Conducting the research involves preparation of the facilities, moderating the group, and gathering the material. After the research has been conducted, the researchers must transcribe the proceedings, code the results, and prepare the report.

Focus group preparation

During the preparation stage of the focus group, methodology researchers meet with management and also staff from departments that have a stake in solving the problem. Qualitative research is conducted when management is exploring new ideas or the cause of a problem. At this meeting a broad, wide-ranging discussion on the issues that management is concerned about should be held. The vaguer the research issue, the more important it is for researchers to clarify what management wants and needs to know.

One of the problems researchers may face in the preparation stage is communicating to management that the focus group discussion must stay 'focused'. Unfortunately, management may have the misconception that an hour-long focus group with eight participants will result in eight hours of information. As a result of this belief, they will give researchers a long list of topics they want covered during the focus group. However, in a focus group only one person can speak at a time, which limits the amount of information that can be gathered. In addition, it is important to remember that besides the time limitation, the purpose of a focus group is to discuss an issue in depth. A focus group should not be conducted as a group survey, where the researcher has a list of questions and then allows each member to respond only quickly. Researchers should come away from the meeting with management with two to three topic areas at most that the focus group will address.

Participant profile

After the research issues have been defined, the participants for the focus group must be chosen. Researchers and management will together develop a participant profile. The profile will describe the desired demographic, psychographic, and geographic characteristics of participants. For example, the research question may ask about the opinions of current customers. In this case, the participants will be chosen to represent the segmentation characteristics of the particular consumer segment the question addresses.

Choose a moderator

After participants have been invited, a moderator must be chosen. If a company or an organization is large enough to support their own marketing research division, the moderator may be someone internal to that company. If not, a moderator must be hired to conduct the focus group. Moderators may be professionals who work in a full-service advertising agency, or they may be consultants with their own company.

The moderator should not be familiar with the participants. In fact, it is best if the moderator has no contact with the participants before the focus group session. Having a pre-existing relationship with a member of the group makes building a rapport with others in the group more difficult. A pre-existing relationship may cause a division in the group between those who know the moderator and those who do not.

Focus group script

The final step in the preparation stage would be to write the focus group script. The script will include the questions that will be asked during the focus group. These main research topic areas will be addressed with general questions that will then lead to additional follow-up questions. The script should be broken down into the three sections of a focus group: building a rapport, probing, and closing. Besides the questions, the script will describe the techniques that will be used to gather information. The technique may be simply a question-and-discussion format. Alternatively, the focus group may use projective techniques. A focus group script may appear deceptively easy to produce. However, to have everyone agree on the final script can take as much effort and time as writing a survey form.

Conducting a focus group

A marketing research firm or large corporation may have a specialized focus group facility. While such a setting is very professional, it is also costly, and it is not necessary to have such a suite of rooms to conduct a successful focus group. In fact, it may be argued that it is counterproductive (Brockhoff 2019). This type of corporate setting is the natural environment of researchers and corporate employees. However, it is not the natural environment of most consumers and many might find it intimidating.

It is possible to have a focus group in any type of location where eight to ten people can be comfortably seated. If technical equipment is needed, it can easily be brought to the location. For example, if a corporation wants to study the needs of young people, it makes more sense to have the focus group in a bar or restaurant where young people congregate. Likewise, people from a specific ethnic group would be more likely to speak candidly if the focus group were held in a community centre in their own neighbourhood. A focus group with children requires special planning to ensure that all legal and ethical requirements are met.

Because of advances in technology, focus groups no longer are limited to having participants in the same location. They may be held online with group members using video with members being able to see each other while they are communicating. The advantage of having the group solely online is that members do not all have to be in the same physical location. An online focus group can also be structured so that the members are not all present at the same time. Instead, the questions can be posted and the members can answer and respond to other answers at their convenience.

Table 6.1 Focus group process

Preparation	Meet with management to clarify issues
	Develop participant profile
	Invite subjects to participate
	Choose moderator
	Write focus group script
Conducting	Prepare facility
	Moderate proceedings
	Gather and maintain information
Analysis	Transcribing information
	Coding information
	Writing report

Technology has been successfully used to conduct quantitative research. Using software to write and distribute a survey online is now considered standard procedure. Digital methods of communication are now also being used to conduct qualitative research, such as interviews and focus groups. In fact, when holding focus groups to discuss the benefits of digital products or the effectiveness of social media promotion, online might be the preferred option. People targeted with digital products and promotion will already be comfortable interacting using technology. They might view the necessity of all being in the same physical location at the same time to share opinions as unnecessarily constricting.

These digital methods of conducting focus groups using website chat rooms of existing groups or links created expressly for the occasion take the place of in-person communication. When using this approach, the research and subject can communicate in real time or the researcher can leave the questions for participants to answer at a time of their convenience. By using webcams or other video technology, people will be able to see and interact with each other and the researcher.

Asynchronous online focus groups are sometimes referred to as bulletin board focus groups. The advantage is that the participants and group moderator do not need to present at the same time. Using methods such as Google Hangouts, the moderator posts questions, to which the focus group members respond (Stewart and Shamdasani 2017). The members also respond to the comments of others, duplicating the interaction that would take place when conducting a focus group in person. Online focus groups can also be conducted synchronously using Skype or some other form of video chat program. This has the advantage of enabling people to see each other body language. The disadvantage is that if the focus group participants live in different time zones, scheduling can be difficult.

These methods try to replicate as closely as possible the personal interaction that takes place face to face. There are advantages to using online methods for focus groups and interviews. First, there are no geographic limitations as to who can be involved. Secondly, people can interact from the comfort of their own home or office. Because they are in familiar surroundings, their reactions may be more natural and honest. Having the focus group or interview online allows the researcher to include photos, images, and video clips for comments. There is also a cost savings because focus groups will not need to be paid for any travel or meal expenses. However, the disadvantage is that the participants are limited to those who have, and are comfortable using, the needed technology.

Focus group stages

A focus group consists of three stages. The first stage is used to build a rapport. This can be accomplished by having the participants give first name introductions. The moderator can then introduce the subject by asking an easy, non-threatening question. Once a rapport has been established, the moderator will move on to more probing questions on the issue. During this portion of the focus group, interaction will be encouraged and follow-up questions will be used. Finally, the moderator will provide a sense of closure by asking a final question or by requesting some last thoughts on the subject.

After the conclusion of the focus group, the moderator will thank the participants for their attendance. Once they have left, it is the moderator's responsibility to maintain all information, including notes and tapes in an orderly fashion. If the focus group was held online, there will be electronic files of everything that is said.

Focus group analysis

After a focus group has been conducted, the final step is to analyse the research findings. This is the responsibility of the moderator, as part of the skill they bring to the role is their ability to interpret what has occurred. The focus group proceedings may have been videoed or taped. In addition, there may be written notes and also material from projective techniques. All the recorded and written information will be analysed by the moderator for common themes and unique insights. After the analysis is completed, a final report will be written. A research report for quantitative techniques will have statistics that are presented in graph or chart form to support its findings. A qualitative research report will rely on supporting its findings using quotes or projective materials. The final task of the moderator is to provide an oral report of the findings.

Moderator

One of the key measures in having a successful focus group is to write a focus group script that addresses the research question. In addition, the subjects must meet the participant profile. Lastly, the right moderator must be selected. A skilled moderator will be able to run a successful focus group even if the subjects aren't as motivated to participate as would be desired and the questions are a bit too vague or too narrow. However, a poor moderator will result in an unsuccessful focus group – even with the most carefully chosen and motivated participants and the most well-written script. Choosing a successful moderator requires paying attention to both personal characteristics and skills.

Desirable personal characteristics

Successful moderators will find the research process interesting. It is not necessary, or even advisable, for them to be knowledgeable about the research topic. However, good researchers continue to find the process of obtaining needed information exciting no matter what topic is under discussion. A moderator will treat each focus group as being important and will be concerned that it provides the information needed by the company or organization. If they do not, they might not be willing to spend the time developing a script and other techniques that will provide the needed information. Instead, they may conduct a focus group using the same procedures and techniques that they used last time for another research project.

A moderator also needs to be comfortable with and feel empathy for the participants. This is especially important if a moderator is of a different age and from a different income level, religion, or ethnicity. Empathy cannot be faked. If focus group participants come from a group whose opinions are usually ignored, they will quickly notice if a moderator does not treat them as equals. For this reason, it is best to have a moderator with at least some similar demographic or psychographic characteristics as participants. If this is not possible, the moderator should have at least worked with similar types of participants in the past.

Required skills

A moderator not only should be familiar with focus groups but should also have at least a basic understanding of all research methodologies. Management is often unclear as to what research method should be used to answer each type of research question. A knowledge of research methodologies will help a moderator to know when the information a company wants would be best discovered through the use of another method.

Table 6.2 Successful moderators

Type of requirement	Essential
Personal characteristics	Interest in research process
	Empathy with participants
Skills and knowledge	Knowledge of research methods
	Competence in group dynamics
	Ability to analyse data and write report

A moderator should also understand group dynamics. They will be unable to direct a group in a productive direction without a strong understanding of how groups function. Finally, a moderator should be skilled in the analysis and reporting of focus group data. Survey data can be analysed by someone who had no input into the design or conducting of a survey. This is not true of a focus group, which is an interactive process between the moderator and the participants.

Handling group conflict

The success of a focus group depends on the interaction between group members. There is no reason that a focus group should not be a pleasant experience with friendly interaction between participants. Of course, not all people have pleasant dispositions. As a result, there may be times when focus group discussion becomes a bit 'heated'. This can be particularly true when sensitive subjects are discussed (Sim and Waterfield 2019). Topics such as religion and politics may be mentioned by participants even though the moderator did not ask for this type of input. A solution to this problem is for the moderator to provide rules at the beginning of the group as to what topics will not be discussed.

One of the causes of having a focus group become confrontational is simply group dynamics. Before a group can work together successfully, there are always some formation issues that must be worked through. An understanding of group dynamics can be helpful in learning to diffuse these conflicts.

Online focus groups

The traditional focus group is conducted with the participants and the moderator sitting around a table with face-to-face personal communication. However, focus groups can take place online, either using text only or also video and audio (Jarvey 2014). Online technology is being adapted for use with focus groups. This includes using existing online communities that attract people who have mutual interests to find participants. This shared interest or lifestyle might vary from a love of comic books to the enjoyment of gourmet foods. Online focus groups are very useful when the research participant profile calls for subjects who have similar psychographic characteristics. A focus group can be conducted 'live', with a moderator posting questions while subjects respond immediately online. Or, the focus group can use a system where questions are posted and subjects can respond at their convenience. At the same time, they can also respond to other participant comments.

An existing online community website can be used to host the focus groups. If plans are for numerous online focus groups, the organization should consider investing in special software used for conducting online focus groups. The advantage of using such software is that it has analytic ability built in. The software will search and find common themes or topics that are mentioned by participants.

Even more importantly than with a traditional focus group, when conducting an online group, the moderator should always identify themselves, the topic of the research, and for whom the research is being conducted. It is unethical for a moderator to conduct research while posing as just another user.

Often members of an online community are eager to communicate their opinions. After all, people who chat online are a self-selected group that wants to communicate. Using this method can be helpful in gaining insights from groups that would not normally attend a traditional focus group. Groups that feel disenfranchised from society, such as the young, ethnic groups, or people who live alternative lifestyles, can be successfully reached with this method.

Using such online sites limits the use of demographic criteria as there is no way to control for gender, age, and economic level. Another consideration when using online focus groups is that this method will not reach a cross-section of everyone interested in a topic. Instead, it will attract only those who are comfortable or interested in communicating online. This will mean that participants are more likely to be younger and better educated. Another disadvantage is that a moderator cannot see the entirety of body language, although the online community is quite skilled at communicating feelings by using both words and facial expressions.

A moderator should have experience in conducting online focus groups because opinions can become extreme when expressed online. In addition, people may adopt a very different persona to the one they use in their everyday lives. Whether the opinions of alternative personas are more or less real is a question best left for psychologists and philosophers. However, moderators need to be aware that extreme opinions may not be acted upon in real life. There are now specialized tools for conducting online focus groups. In this case, participants come online specifically to participate in a focus group.

Videoconferencing focus groups

One of the disadvantages of holding online focus groups is that there is no way to record nonverbal communication. Using a videoconferencing platform such as Zoom to conduct focus groups overcomes this problem. Larger research firms may have specialized facilities used for videoconferencing focus groups. These can reduce the expense of bringing the moderator and participants together in one location. Videoconferencing has the advantage of allowing the participants and moderators to see each other. They can therefore react to each other's body language and communicate more effectively. A sophisticated videoconferencing system allows all the members to see everyone's reactions to each other even when they are in many different locations. Another advantage of videoconferencing is that it allows products that are the subject of research to be shown and some projective techniques can also be used.

The disadvantage comes in that focus group participants must be familiar with the software platform and have the equipment and bandwidth. Even if they do not all participants would feel comfortable communicating using this method. It might take a while for participants to feel comfortable enough to actively participate. There may also be some discomfort among participants with videoing from the home computer to a moderator who is a stranger. However, an incentive may be effective in overcoming this hesitancy.

Discussion questions

1   What are the advantages and disadvantages of using focus groups to explore consumer preferences?
2   How would you answer the claim that focus groups are not useful because too few participants are involved?
4   What argument would you present to management for the expense of conducting both a focus group and a survey?
5   Why should both management and researchers be involved in the development of a participant profile?
6   Why would moderators be able to obtain better data when they have empathy for the research subjects?
7   Which is more important to a focus group's success a skilled moderator or the right participants?
8   What would be the advantages and disadvantages of using an online focus group to discuss older consumers' purchasing of travel tours?

Answer these questions to continue creating a marketing research plan

1   What questions will be asked during the focus group?
2   How will the group moderator be chosen?
3   Where will the focus group be held?

References

Brockhoff, Libby. "How to Get Focus Groups out of the 1950's." *Forbes*. January 24, 2019. www.forbes.com/sites/forbesagencycouncil/2019/01/24/how-to-get-focus-groups-out-of-the-1950s/?sh=5d42435a48a4. Accessed April 5, 2021.

Jarvey, Nichole. "Focus Groups: Marketing's Oldest Technique Adapts to a Digital Age." *Digital Current*. July 14, 2014. www.digitalcurrent.com/blog/focus-groups-in-digital-age/ Accessed January 30, 2021.

Sim, Julius and Jackie Waterfield. "Focus Group Methodology: Some Ethical Challenges." *Quality & Quantity*. July 16, 2019. https://link.springer.com/article/10.1007/s11135-019-00914-5. Accessed February 2, 2021.

Stewart, D. and P. Shamdasani. "Online Focus Groups." *Journal of Advertising*, 2017, 46(1): 48–60.

Stromberg, Joseph. "Focus Groups Shape What we Buy. But How Much do they Really Say About Us?." *Vox*. January 22, 2019. www.vox.com/the-goods/2019/1/22/18187443/focus-groups-brand-market-research. Accessed April 13, 2021.

7 Interviews, observation, and projective techniques

Interviews

Interviewing is a qualitative research technique using personal communication between a researcher and a research subject. The purpose of conducting interviews includes gaining insights into consumer behaviour, obtaining factual information, and developing hypotheses for quantitative research. Besides in-depth one-to-one interviewing between researchers and research subjects to gain insights on consumer preferences, researchers may also conduct intercept interviews. Intercept interviews are given to numerous participants using only three to four quick questions and are given by researchers at locations where specific subjects can be found. While the same questions will be asked to all participants, the method does allow for very limited follow-up questioning.

The purpose of research interviews is to explore ideas, gain knowledge, or develop hypotheses that can then be tested using quantitative research. Research interviews use a partially structured approach to questioning. Some of the questions will be asked verbatim of each research subject. A researcher will determine other questions to ask as the interview progresses. The fact that some of the questions are the same for each research participant allows comparability. At the same time, a researcher can also add additional questions, which allows flexibility. The fact that interview methodology may be only partially structured does not mean that the interview process can be treated casually, as an interview is not simply a conversation. A researcher must spend time carefully preparing research questions if an interview is to be successful.

Interview stages

In-depth interviews go through four stages. All start with an opening phase where introductions are made and the purpose of the research is explained. Then, it is a short questioning phase that includes easily answered,

DOI: 10.4324/9781003165194-8

predetermined questions about a participant's consumer behaviour or opinions. In the probing phase, follow-up questions based on the responses received during the questioning phase are asked. During the closing stage, a researcher will thank a participant and answer any questions they may have about what will happen to the information they have provided.

Research interviewing stages

* Opening: communicates the purpose of interview and establishes trust.
* Questioning: uses predetermined questions.
* Probing: uses follow-up questions based on earlier responses.
* Closing: researcher thanks the participant and answers the participant's questions.

Advantages of using interviews

Interview methodology has the advantage of allowing research participants to express ideas in their own words. Because of the length of an interview a participant is allowed time to develop their ideas fully. If a researcher is still unclear as to a participant's meaning, he or she can ask probing follow-up questions. Interviews are also used for gathering information that can be developed into a hypothesis that can be tested in turn by using quantitative research. Finally, the interviews can be useful for gathering specific factual knowledge.

Interviews can also be conducted online. This has the advantage of not having to travel to another location to conduct the interview. There are disadvantages to online interviews (Jiang 2020). They can be draining to conduct as the brain has to spend more time interpreting non-verbal cues. Body language can communicate as much information as words. They can also result in less information being obtained as people can feel that being watched in a personal space, such as their home, is an invasion of privacy.

Types of Interviews

The choice of marketing research interviewing methodologies includes in-depth interviews. With this technique, a researcher spends most of the interview exploring consumer motivation and behaviour. Intercept interviews are short person-on-the-street interviews that only ask a few predetermined questions. This information can be used to develop hypotheses that can then be proved or disproved by using quantitative research.

In-depth interviews are conducted between an interviewer and a single participant. The interview is partially structured with some of the questions being predetermined. These questions are written by researchers and based on the research question. A researcher will ask other questions based on information provided by the participants during the interviews. In-depth interviews usually last a little under an hour and go through four phases: opening, questioning, probing, and closing. During the 'opening' phase an interviewer will explain to a participant the purpose of the research. Once this is concluded the research will move into the 'questioning' phase. The questions will start by being very general in nature and then will move on to more specific information.

Sometimes research questions will touch on sensitive issues. Some industries, such as health care, personal products, and life insurance, often need to conduct research that asks participants questions about difficult times in their lives. Interviewers for these types of research projects need to have special training so that the research does not leave any emotional scars. If conducted with sensitivity, research participants may find the interview process therapeutic rather than harmful.

Intercept or person-on-the-street interviews also ask open-ended questions. In this case though the interview is kept very short. An intercept interview should only take a few minutes and is therefore limited to three or four questions. The participants are chosen and interviewed at the location where they can be found. This technique is often used when the subjects needed for the research are unwilling to agree to an in-depth interview. Because the interviews take a short period of time, many more can be conducted. However, the short time period for person-on-the-street interviews means that there isn't time for in-depth probing questions. Interviewers used for this type of interview do not need the same level of technical skill. Instead, it is more important that the potential participants view the interviewer as someone who is friendly and approachable.

Table 7.1 Example of in-depth interview structure

Opening phase	The researcher explains the purpose of the research concerns: breakfast cereal preferences
Questioning phase	What brand do you eat? (predetermined)
Probing phase	Why do you prefer this brand? (predetermined)
Follow-up questions based on probing responses	What do you mean by 'not so sweet'? (unstructured) Why do you think the brand is 'good for you'? (unstructured)
Closing phase	Thanks for your participation. Do you have any questions about today's interview?

Types of questions

Types of interview questions include descriptive, causal, consequence, and non-directional. Descriptive questions ask for facts concerning behaviour. Such questions are usually both easy to ask and easy to answer. Causal questions ask research subjects to think about why a certain behaviour takes place. These questions ask for underlying motivations and take more time and thought to answer. Even more difficult are consequence questions. These types of questions ask research subjects to construct a hypothetical example in their mind and to then respond on how they would act. Non-directional questions ask research participants to determine if there is a relationship between two facts.

Participants

Because interviews are a qualitative process, it can sometimes be forgotten that as much care should be taken when selecting participants who fit the profile as when designing a sample for a quantitative survey. It is true that it is generally more difficult to have a potential participant agree to an interview than a survey because of the time involved. Therefore, researchers may be tempted to focus more on who is willing to be interviewed rather than who fits the profile. Unfortunately, if the research subjects for interviews are not carefully selected, both time and money will be wasted. A willing, but inappropriate participant will result in not obtaining the needed information and the interview will be wasted.

A company's management along with researchers will have to meet to determine a participant profile. First, they must decide if they want to interview current customers, potential customers, or both. They must then decide on the demographic and psychographic profile of the subjects. The profile should be very specific, and the researchers involved should explain to management if extra time will be needed to recruit appropriate research subjects.

Observational research

Another research method that can be used by organizations is observation. Observational research is based on analysing what people do rather than what they say. The research is conducted without communicating with people but rather by noting how they act. Observational research is being conducted in new ways as technology is now making it possible to 'observe' using the internet, scanner-tracking, video, and neuroimaging.

Advantages of observational research

Observational research allows researchers to conduct studies without directly involving research subjects. Using this technique can confirm what people do rather than what they say they do. Observational research can also expand perspectives without spending money on more expensive research. In addition, the research subjects do not need to answer questions about actions that they might find difficult to recall.

An important advantage of conducting observational research is that it will determine what people do versus what they say they do. Consumer behaviour is not static but is constantly evolving as people react to changes in the external environment (Rogers 2020). Research subjects may give inaccurate information when surveyed about their actions or choices because they might recall incorrectly what they did either because of inattention or because of poor memory. Observational research of museum visitors may find that they spent the majority of their time in the gift shop and café. Another occasion for conducting an observational research study is when the research subjects may not remember their actions, such as families after a busy day at an amusement park.

Types of observations

There are three distinct types of observational research. When using the complete observer approach, research subjects will not be aware they are under observation. Using another type of observation, researchers will participate in the behaviour at the same time as they are observing. A third approach is for researchers to completely immerse themselves in a behaviour.

When using the complete observer approach, a researcher will have no interaction with participants. Using this method, the marketing researcher should attempt to be invisible to the participants. This can be accomplished by being hidden from view. In this case, the researcher may be watching from a location outside the sightline of customers or even using video. If this is not possible, the marketing researcher will try to be almost invisible by not being noticed by the research subjects. The researcher can stand behind a counter so they will be thought to be just another clerk. This type of observation is conducted when the presence of the researcher may change the actions of those being observed (e.g., if a marketing researcher wants to observe children at play, but the presence of an unfamiliar researcher would affect how the children interact).

Another type of observation has researchers participating in the behaviour that is being observed. This type of observation is used when it is impossible to conceal an observer if the researcher needs a deeper understanding of the cause of the behaviour (Ross 2018). In some social settings, the use of a silent person observing would draw others' notice. Even a silent observer taking notes might result in calls to the local police. Being a participant also allows the researcher to question the participant if they do not understand the reason for the observed action or choice.

A third way of conducting observation is for the researcher to be a complete participant. With this method, a researcher engages in the same consumer behaviour as the research subjects. If an airline wants to learn more about the experience of being a passenger on a shuttle flight, a researcher can travel on that flight as just another commuting passenger. They will not only be able to observe but also be able to overhear comments. Because researchers can blend into the action, they don't have to worry that their presence is distorting the behaviour of the research subjects around them.

Designing the observational research process

Observational research involves more than just watching people. If research findings are to be useful, it is important that the research methodology is carefully designed and that trained observational researchers are used. Once a research question has been written, the determination must be made as to which members of the entire research population will be observed. The next step in the process is to determine exactly what should be observed. This question is just as important as asking what questions should be included on a survey form or writing a script for a focus group. If the wrong behaviour is observed, the findings will be useless.

Observation is difficult. It requires patience, attention to detail, and the ability to be unobtrusive. When selecting observers, it is important to consider whether they have the patience to sit or stand quietly while watching others. If someone does not have the necessary patience, no amount of training will correct this. However, training can help observers to pay attention to detail and learn to be unobtrusive.

A well-designed observation form will help to keep an observer watching what needs to be observed rather. An observation form that uses the systematic recording of specific types of behaviour during specific time periods will help a researcher stay focused on the important details that are needed to answer a research question.

Projective techniques

Projective techniques are used to encourage communication using nonverbal methods of response. They are used when it is difficult for participants to verbally express their feelings. They also provide interaction that will help maintain participant interest during other research methods. They include completion tasks and other techniques such as card sorts and thematic appreciation tests. These techniques elicit information through writing, drawing, and a variety of ways other than answering verbally. These techniques, borrowed from psychology, are gaining increased use in marketing. Such projective techniques aim to gain insights from participants of which they may not be totally aware. These techniques can be used alone or as part of another research methodology.

Advantages of using projective techniques

Projective techniques are usually combined with other research methods. An advantage of combining the use of projective techniques with other methods, such as focus groups or interviews, is that they provide an additional means of gathering information. Projective techniques have the advantage of obtaining information of which participants may not be fully aware. They also allow shy or quiet participants to take part without speaking. Another advantage of using projective techniques is to gain information on topics that a participant may be unwilling to discuss. Having these opinions expressed anonymously by having them written allows participants to express views they might not state out loud.

The use of projective techniques makes research sessions more interactive and interesting. In today's technology-driven world, where people have immediate information and entertainment at the press of a button, sitting still while a topic is being discussed can be difficult. Unless the research participants are very interested in the topic, they may find an hour-long focus group rather boring. Projective techniques can be used not just to gather data that cannot be obtained in any other way but also to keep the research session more interesting. If participants are bored, they will not provide the necessary information, while an interactive environment will result in richer data.

Types of projective techniques

There are many different projective techniques that researchers can use individually or in combination with other research methods. These are creative tools that are especially appealing to researchers working in non-profit organizations and creative industries. The most common projective techniques are completion tasks, such as word associations, sentence and story completion, and cartoons. Creative researchers may develop their own techniques.

Word association is simply asking for a participant's first response to a name, photo, or event. The idea is to get emotional, rather than intellectual, responses. Word association can be used with individuals or in focus groups or interviews. One example of its use would be if a business was planning a redesign of their store. A researcher, rather than just describe the store, may show a photo to a focus group and ask the participants to write the first three words that come to mind. Using this technique, a researcher could also show participants a product or photo of a place. The participants must then record their answers on small cards which are gathered up by the researcher. Alternatively, participants may be asked to record their answers on large sheets of paper so that they can be immediately shared with others. Words that might be listed when participants are asked about a new store design are 'exciting', 'confusing', 'boring', 'crowded', 'lovely', 'feminine', or 'manly'.

An example of a sentence completion task would be to have the participants complete a sentence on their motivation for choosing a new product. If the research is being conducted regarding a service, participants might be asked to complete a sentence about a happy or unhappy customer that uses this service. Sentence completion allows for comparison between participant responses. Some responses to the sentences might express the fact that the Corner Cafe is a fun place where people can socialize. Other participants might answer that the Corner Cafe is a place where people drink too much and make trouble. These negative views might not be expressed using other methods. Researchers can then compare the demographic profiles of those participants who expressed negative views.

Story completion is a bit more challenging for participants. They will be asked to finish a story that a researcher has prepared. For example, story completion could be used when researching how young people view a university. The participants in this research would be current students who might have difficultly when questioned about why they decided to attend that university. A more creative and interesting technique would present them with the following story. To see if opinions about the university would vary because of gender, the name Tom could be substituted. If researchers wanted to see if the story would change by ethnicity or religion, the names Anu, Pierre, Jacob, or Mohammed could be substituted.

Cartoons can also be used as a means for participants to communicate ideas nonverbally. Cartoons can be used to enable participants to, almost literally, put their words into someone else's mouth. This can save a participant from the potential embarrassment of stating opinions in front of strangers who may disagree. Another advantage of this technique is that it can make responding to a question more fun. The cartoon usually consists of two characters with speech bubbles over their heads like those in comic books. One character's speech bubble will ask a question; the other character will have an empty speech bubble in which the participant will put a response. One character might be saying, 'Hi Alan, I was thinking of visiting the new cafe. Want to go?' The survey participants will then put their own answers into the other speech bubble. This allows them to communicate their own ideas through someone else. It also assists participants in responding by helping them to picture the circumstances. When using cartoon completion, the characters shown in the cartoon can be varied by age, gender, or ethnicity. This can be used to see if the responses vary based on the consumer characteristics shown in the cartoon. In addition, the same characters can be used but the product being shown can be varied. This allows researchers to compare and contrast responses based on demographic or psychographic characteristics.

Process

Using projective techniques requires preparation just as any other form of research does. First, an idea must be created that will help to answer a research question. Projective techniques should not be used simply to engage the attention of participants. Instead, each technique should obtain the information that will help to answer a research question. Once an idea has been created, materials must be prepared. These might include cartoons, drawings, half-completed ads, cards, or any other suitable material. A little creativity and a computer will allow a researcher to find or create interesting and useful materials.

When projective techniques are used, a researcher must explain the reasons for using the technique without leading participants as to what to create. This can be difficult, as participants may look to a researcher to provide the 'right' answer. While people understand how to answer questions verbally, answering them nonverbally may be a new experience. If a researcher finds a group unwilling to cooperate, they must be ready with a different technique for obtaining the required information.

Once the research is completed, a researcher must gather and label all the information. The names of participants aren't important, but their characteristics and the date of the research should be noted as this will help in the analysis of the data. The data will be examined for the range of responses provided, with the researcher noting common themes and unusual insights. The completed projective material can be very useful when preparing a final report. Drawings can be reproduced and used in the body of the report or else included in the appendix, while quotes provided through sentence completion may be used verbatim. These examples of projective techniques provide a unique insight into the research subject's thinking.

Table 7.2 Ranked important factors when choosing qualitative research subjects

Focus groups	Interviews	Observation	Ethnography
Personal characteristics	Research issue knowledge	Location	Group affinity
Location	Personal characteristics	Personal characteristics	Comfort with technology
Research issue knowledge	Location	Research issue knowledge	Willingness to participate

Ethnographic research

Ethnography is a research technique originally used by anthropologists and sociologists to gather information on how groups of people interact daily. Rather than ask questions or simply observe, a researcher becomes one of the members of that specific group for a period of time. This allows researchers to more clearly understand the values and attitudes that underlie a group's behaviour (Burrows 2014). Market researchers use ethnography to better understand consumers' lifestyles, attitudes, and product use. Its purpose is to gain a deeper understanding of consumers by studying how they live rather than only asking for their ideas and opinions.

Ethnographic marketing research studies how consumers use products and can take place in a research subject's home or at their place of employment, although gaining access to conduct research in these settings may be difficult. While a researcher is involved with a group, they will be keeping track of behaviours by preparing notes and, if possible, gathering photographic or video evidence.

For example, a company that designs office furniture might wish to market a new type of office desk. Rather than use a survey or focus group to ask what features employees might like, the researcher concerned could conduct ethnographic research to learn how employees use office furniture. To conduct the study, this researcher would remain in the worksite, taking notes, talking to key individuals, and gathering visual data. The research might reveal that office workers do not have a convenient place to set their cups of coffee and lack a desk area where they can work jointly.

This type of research can now be conducted by the participant rather than have a researcher present (West 2018). Using a cell phone, the research participant can photograph or video research subjects. These can be later analysed by the researcher. Another method would be to design an app that the participant would use to record their activities with the researcher viewing the results in real time. A webcam could also be used as a passive device to record and analyse behaviour.

Ethnography is used to research groups that would not, or could not, participate in traditional research studies. These groups might be based on lifestyle or demographic factors such as religion or ethnicity. Another rationale for using ethnography is to gather details of behaviour that are so engrained into the fabric of everyday life that they are difficult for people to describe. For example, if researchers want to know how families do their laundry so that a better container for laundry detergent can be designed, they can stay with a family on laundry day. The company can then use this information to make strategic decisions and to build a stronger relationship with consumers.

Advantages of conducting ethnographic research

The advantage of conducting ethnographic research is that researchers not only observe but also share the experience with research subjects. Ethnography therefore provides insights that cannot be gained from merely observing or discussing. In addition, ethnography research is a valuable tool to use when researching consumers in other cultures where individuals may be reluctant to state their opinions directly to a stranger as it is not considered appropriate.

One disadvantage of conducting ethnographic research is that it takes time to develop the necessary trust to gain access to a group or family to conduct the research. In order to allow for a behaviour to unfold naturally, the research time will need to be longer than for other types of research. In addition, this process must use researchers skilled in this technique so that useful marketing information can be obtained.

Process of conducting ethnographic research

The first step in designing an ethnographic study is to determine the group and the behaviour that are to be researched. The most important decision will be to decide upon the location where this research will take place. The location might be in a store, at home, in the workplace, or at a place where the research subjects socialize. In addition, researchers must establish trust with the members of the group that is to be observed. Because the researchers may be entering the private space of the research subjects, taking the time to establish trust is imperative. To establish trust, both the purpose of the research and the research process should be carefully and fully explained.

Using ethnographic research, a researcher both watches and listens the subjects under study. If the observation reveals that there are key individuals in a group that are of interest, informal interviews may take place to obtain more information. Besides watching and listening, a visual record of photos or videotapes may also be taken. All the data are then analysed for common behavioural patterns and why these patterns exist.

Ethnographic research process

- Decide on the research subjects and behaviour to be studied.
- Gain their permission and build up trust.
- Observe the individuals and the group.
- Informally interview key individuals.
- If needed, photograph or video the behaviour.
- Analyse the written and visual data.

Participant involvement in ethnographic research

A unique aspect of ethnographic research is participant involvement. This can be accomplished by having participants complete logs or diaries or using photography. Research subjects can be asked to keep a log of their actions that can then be analysed. For example, a fast-food restaurant chain may wish to know more about the lunchtime habits of office workers. The restaurant's management may believe that business is falling because more people are taking shorter lunch periods while working at their desks. One method to gain insights is to ask workers to participate in a study where they log in how long they take for lunch each day. Diaries will ask for more detailed recorded information. For example, teenage girls may be asked to keep a diary of their clothing purchases that also records how they feel about the items bought.

An advantage of combining logs or diaries with ethnographic research is that it can track a research subject's behaviour over time. The disadvantage is that it is difficult to have people maintain their interest in recording the data in a timely fashion. If they do not, they are likely to go back and fill in entries for previous days with estimated information. However, this method can easily be adapted to online use, which makes the entire process much easier. A research subject can either log on to a website where they will record the information each day or they can email the researcher with the information. If they forget, the researcher can email them a reminder.

Another method to have research subjects become involved as researchers is to provide them with either digital or video cameras. They can then record objects or interactions that they feel are important. For example, children might be asked to photograph their favourite toys at home. This material is then provided to the researchers for analysis.

Discussion questions

1 Why could it be argued that a research study on alcohol use should use interviews rather than focus groups?
2 What different types of questions would be asked during the questioning and probing stages of the above interview?
3 Why are projective techniques sometimes used in focus groups?
4 What type of projective technique could be used to encourage participation by quiet members?
5 What type of observation could be used for a study to know what people shop for food at a market?
6 What type of online communities would help with when conducting ethnographic research on the purchase of athletic equipment?

Answer these questions to continue creating a marketing research plan

1 What interview questions will be asked?
2 Which behaviour could be studied using observational research?
3 Which types of projective techniques would be useful in encouraging interaction?
4 What online communities could be studied to answer the research question?

References

Burrows, David. "How to Use Ethnography for In-depth Consumer Insight." *Marketing Week*. www.marketingweek.com/2014/05/09/how-to-use-ethnography-for-in-depth-consumer-insight/. Accessed March 31, 2021.

Jiang, Manyu. "The Reason Why Zoom Calls Drain Your Energy." *BBC*. April 22, 2020. www.bbc.com/worklife/article/20200421-why-zoom-video-chats-are-so-exhausting. Accessed April 24, 2021.

Rogers, Charlotte. "Helen Edwards: Marketers are Underestimating the Signs of Customer Behaviour." *Marketing Week*. 2020. www.marketingweek.com/helen-edwards-signs-behaviour-science/. Accessed March 2, 2021.

Ross, Jim. "The Role of Observation in User Research." *CXMatters*. September 10, 2018. www.uxmatters.com/mt/archives/2018/09/the-role-of-observation-in-user-research.php. Accessed March 14, 2021.

West, Rebecca. "Methods of Mobile Ethnography." *Civicom*. November 7, 2018. https://insights.civicommrs.com/methods-of-mobile-ethnography. Accessed February 24, 2021.

8 Analysing research results

Analysing data process

The data from quantitative research are in the form of numbers that can be totalled, averaged, compared, and contrasted. The resulting statistics are used to describe consumer behaviour or preference within a targeted population segment. Management may not understand how the statistics were obtained, but they can easily understand the averages and percentages and, therefore, trust the resulting information.

In contrast, qualitative research results in verbal data and images including recordings, written words, and sometimes photos or videos. These data cannot be statistically manipulated, compared, and contrasted. In addition, the analysis does not result in easily understood percentages. For this reason, management may well misunderstand and mistrust the resulting analysis. Rather than proving facts using statistics, the analysis of qualitative data has as its focus the search for meanings. This is because qualitative research is used to answer the question of 'Why?' The answer will always be more complicated to explain to management than just a percentage or an average.

When analysing all types of data, there is a danger of becoming caught up in the process. It should be remembered that the amount of data and the time spent on analysis should correlate with the importance of the decision (Hermann 2020). There is no possibility of being assured that any resulting recommendation will be 100 per cent accurate. If the action from the recommendation can be quickly changed if the results are not what is expected, then less time can be spent on analysis. If the recommendation will take the organization in a direction from which it will be difficult to change, then more analysis should be conducted.

Differences in analysis

* *Quantitative analysis*
  * Statistics that describe behaviour.

DOI: 10.4324/9781003165194-9

- Analysis of quantitative data occurs after research has been completed.
- Statistics are manipulated for new meanings.

- *Qualitative analysis*

  - Recommendations based on concepts and categories.
  - Analysis of data occurs while research is still being conducted.
  - Data are repeatedly analysed by researchers for new insights.

Qualitative research, as with quantitative research, is conducted to answer a research question. However, a skilled qualitative researcher may find more in the data than just the answer to a research question. Quantitative research is usually conducted using a survey methodology. This limits the responses of participants to the issues on the survey form. Because the subjects involved in qualitative research can provide any additional information, which they feel is important, there will be a wealth of data. These data may provide new insights to help answer the research question. In fact, it may turn out that the subjects have an entirely different view of the solution to a problem or an idea for a new opportunity (Madsbjerg and Rasmussen 2014). This can result in an entirely new understanding of the relationship between the customer and the product that could be achieved through the analysis of quantitative data.

Data organization

Data organization involves both the collection and the transformation of the collected information. Organization of data according to research question can be particularly important for qualitative research, as the findings may need to be compared with the findings from quantitative data on the same subject. Some of the data resulting from the research might be lists that have been collected on large pieces of paper on collected on an online site. Focus groups commonly use this method so that everyone present can view the responses being provided to questions asked by the moderator. The lists are commonly written in marker pen in large print and then hung on walls around the room or posted online where everyone can see. The information on these lists must be labelled and dated. Each label should include the research question that resulted in the list of information. The date of the focus group and the name of the researcher should also be noted on each collected list.

Table 8.1 Organization of data

Research method	Organization principle
Focus groups	Research question and group
Projective techniques	Technique
Interviews	Topic
Observation	Location
Ethnography	Organized by online community

Transcribing recordings

Qualitative interviews and focus groups will both result in tape recordings that will need to be transcribed. If possible, a word-for-word transcription should be produced. However, if there is a great deal of taped material, this may not be economically feasible. A good transcript will allow a company to experience the research process as if they were there.

It is best if the researcher who moderated the focus groups or conducted the interviews listens to the tape before transcription. While they are busy conducting the research, it is always difficult for a researcher to retain all the information that is being shared. Listening to the tape will refresh a researcher's memory of what was said. In addition, the tone of voice used and even the silences between speech can provide insights.

Quantitative analysis process

Qualitative marketing research methods analyse consumers' psychographic characteristics, including attitudes, opinions, values, and ideas. These characteristics are difficult to express using numbers. On the other hand, quantitative marketing research methods analyse consumers' current or future behaviour which can be expressed using numbers or percentages. When analysing the data from quantitative research, consumers' physical characteristics, such as gender, age, religion, ethnicity, income, education level, or even their height, hair colour, or weight, can be quantified. In addition, consumers' behaviour can be quantified by frequency of purchase, consistency of purchase, place of purchase, or size of purchase. Using statistical analysis researchers will explain behaviour using numbers rather than words. Furthermore, if the sample for a population is sufficiently large and properly selected, researchers will be able to say with some certainty that the research findings are probably true for the total population.

After a survey has been conducted, researchers will be faced with either a pile of survey forms or, if the survey was conducted online, an electronic file. Researchers must now begin the task of analysing the data. This process of data analysis will begin with a pre-analysis stage, where researchers will review the data for its validity, completeness, and accuracy. They will then code any open-ended questions and enter all the data into a computer software program if it was not conducted online. The electronic file still needs to be reviewed for completeness, and any responses to open-ended questions must be coded. This is also true of online forms that ask for complaints or suggestions.

Data analysis using descriptive statistics

Once the data have been entered into the computer software program, marketing researchers are now ready to start the process of analysing the data. They should never forget that the purpose of the analysis is to provide information that can be used for making strategic decisions. There are two types of statistical analysis that can be used, and these are descriptive and inferential. Descriptive analysis collects, summarizes, and presents a set of data. This type of analysis is simple for researchers to conduct and for management to understand.

It needs to be remembered that analysis is a multi-step process. The first stage provides the researcher with data. These are the raw numbers that are totalled from the survey. Alone, they are not helpful. The next step is to turn the data into information by understanding what they mean to the company or organization conducting the research. This information should result in an answer to the research question (Dykes 2016). The final step is the most important, which is to develop insights as to what the answer to the research question means. The research can only be considered successful if it results in actionable steps that should be taken to solve the research problem.

Descriptive statistics help researchers to see patterns in research data. A basic concept used to analyse consumer characteristics and behaviour is frequency, including one-way frequency and cross tabulation. Using frequency researchers can identify how many participants' responses were similar. Cross tabulation compares the relationship between the responses to two different questions. Another concept is central tendency, which includes the mode, median, and mean. In addition, dispersion of central tendency must be examined, including range, variance, and standard deviation.

Descriptive statistics

* Frequency: one-way, cross-tabulation.
* Central tendency: mode, median, mean.
* Dispersion: range, variance, standard deviation.

Frequency can be understood using the example of a survey question that asked why consumers shopped at a particular store. The survey question may have provided three answers to choose from of good prices, the best selection, and helpful service. Frequency counts how many participants choose each answer. Cross-tabulation shows how the data collected in the survey are related. If the survey had also asked participants' age, the data could be analysed to see if age made a difference in the answer.

Central tendency includes the concept of average. People often use the term 'average' when they are referring to a middle ranking. However, there are several ways to measure average or central tendency that include mode, median, and mean. Mode refers to the response that is the most common for all participants. Mode is used when describing nominal data, which can have one of either two states of being, but not both. Median is the response that measures the halfway point of the responses. Median is used in ordinal data, where there is a degree of difference. Mean is the average of all the responses. The mean is calculated by adding all the responses and then dividing by the number of participants.

Dispersion measures

One of the issues that researchers must analyse is how varied the responses are from the calculated mean. To do so researchers use the concepts of range, variance, and standard deviation. Range is the easiest dispersion measure to understand and tells researchers how widely answers are dispersed. To calculate range, the smallest value expressed in the survey is subtracted from the highest value. This gives the range of responses. The variance of the set of numbers around the mean helps researchers to understand how dispersed each individual response is from the mean.

Standard deviation

The higher the variance, the more dispersed are the responses in the set of data. The problem with the variance number is that being squared, the number no longer has any meaning. If the square root of the variance is calculated, the answer will be the standard deviation, which is in the same units, currency, as the original numbers.

If the standard deviation is added and then subtracted from the variance, this tells researchers that this range is where most responses will fall. If the standard deviation is greater in one data set than the other, then the responses provided by the participants in that sample will have varied more widely. While this is easy to see in a small sample of ten numbers, it would not be easy to see in a set of 950 numbers. If these standard deviation numbers are then added and subtracted from the mean, they will show where most of the responses lie.

Data analysis using inferential statistics

The other type of statistical analysis that researchers can conduct uses inferential statistics. These statistical methods go beyond just describing the data discovered during the research. Of course, no marketing research study that uses a sample can 'prove' anything with absolute certainty. What the analysis of quantitative research data can do, however, indicates whether a hypothesis is most likely to be false. Using inferential statistics, researchers can perform statistical tests to determine if responses from a sample can be used to draw conclusions about an entire population. In fact, more than one statistical test can be conducted on the same set of data.

Statistical testing process

The first step in using statistical analysis to indicate the truth of a hypothesis is to state the hypothesis, or guess, about some characteristics of consumers or their behaviour. The research methodology will then be designed to ensure that these characteristics, whether about people or their behaviour, are measured. Once the research study has been completed and the data are entered onto a computer, the measured variable for the sample of participants will be compared with the expected outcome stated in the hypothesis.

The type of test that will be used to determine if the difference is significant depends on both the type of measurement that was used and the type of resulting data. These tests can be used on their own or in combination. The z-test is used to determine if the differences in proportions or mean of characteristics are statistically significant or not, while the t-test also looks for statistical significance but between the means of two unrelated groups. The z-test is used in marketing when one segment of consumers is being studied.

Testing the hypothesis

A hypothesis is a guess that is made by the company or individuals commissioning the research. The research question may be whether to spend money to develop and introduce a new product. Qualitative research has indicated that many consumers would be interested in this product. However, the finance department of the company has stated that at least 20 per cent of current customers will need to purchase the product to make it financially viable.

This first hypothesis is the null hypothesis and will be stated as what the company does not wish to be true. (The symbol H_0 is used to designate the null hypothesis.) The null hypothesis is considered true until proven false. For the company in this example the null hypothesis is that less than 20 per cent of current customers will be interested in purchasing the product. The alternative hypothesis would be that 20 per cent or more will be interested in purchasing the product. (The alternative hypothesis is designated H_1.) One hypothesis is the opposite of the other and so both cannot be true.

The statistical tests cannot be used to prove the hypothesis true. This is impossible as the only way to know with 100 per cent accuracy if a hypothesis is true is to survey the entire population. If the null hypothesis is proved false, then the alternative hypothesis (that 20 per cent or more of customers will be interested) can be accepted as being true. The null hypothesis needs to be expressed in such a way that its rejection leads to the acceptance of the preferred conclusion – developing the new product.

The publishing company surveyed a sample of 1,100 customers (more than the sample size of 1,024 that would have been needed to make the study valid at 95 per cent confidence) and found that 22 per cent stated they were interested. While this is over the required 20 per cent, researchers know that taking a sample will never be as accurate as asking everyone. However, the question remains that if 22 per cent is so close, then is it simply an error that made it over 20 per cent?

Therefore, the next step is to calculate whether the difference between the hypothesized outcome and the survey outcome is statistically significant. While the word 'significant' usually means important, in statistics it means 'true'. The test to find if it is significant would be automatically calculated by a statistical computer software program. However, the formula is actually easy to understand. To calculate the significance all that is needed is three numbers: the hypothesized percentage, the sample percentage, and the standard error of the percentage. Researchers already have two of these: the hypothesized and sample percentages. To calculate the standard error of the percentage, the researcher would use the following formula.

A rough calculation of standard error can be done by remembering the standard numbers for confidence levels. For a 95 per cent confidence level, the number was 1.96 and for 97 per cent confidence 2.58. The z-score tells the researchers whether they can say with 95 or 97 per cent confidence to start production of the new product.

Level of confidence

The possibility that the null hypothesis will be rejected as false when it is indeed true is called a Type I error, which is signified by using the lower-case Greek alpha (α). The amount of possibility that a Type I error has been committed is called the level of significance of the statistical test. Researchers must decide on the amount of risk they are willing to tolerate of committing a Type I error. There are standard levels of risk that are considered acceptable when conducting statistical analysis. These standard levels, or value of α, are 0.01, 0.05, or 0.010. Another way to express these values is that there is a 1 per cent, 5 per cent, or 10 per cent chance of the hypothesis being rejected when it is indeed true. The traditional value used by researchers is 0.05, or there is a 5 per cent risk that the null hypothesis is false, but it isn't rejected.

Another type of error, Type II, happens when the null hypothesis is not rejected when it should be. The Greek letter beta (β) is used for this type of error. A statistical test to check for Type I errors is called a one-tailed test, while a statistical test to check for Type II errors is called a two-tailed test. Most researchers will only use a one-tailed test.

Chi-square tests

The Chi-square test is used for what is called 'goodness-of-fit' when analysing frequencies of responses in a frequency table using cross-tabulation. Marketers often want to know if a there is a relationship between a specific group of consumers and some preference for a product benefit. Marketers also may want to know if men or women prefer the product in a smaller-size bottle. While this statement could be presented as hypothesis, this is not necessary. In fact, when using Chi-square all that researchers need to do is think – the computer will handle the rest. The computer, based on the proportion of men to women in the sample, will calculate what the expected percentages would be if there was no difference in preference versus if gender makes a difference.

It would be simple to compare these numbers using percentages if the groups were all the same size. However, this is unlikely to be true. For this reason, the Chi-square test can be used to determine if there is a statistically valid difference in the relationship between age and reason.

Table 8.2 Data analysis process

Stage	Tasks
Pre-analysis	Review data for validity, completeness, and accuracy
	Code open-ended questions
	Enter the data into a computer software program
Analysis of responses using descriptive statistics	Calculate: Frequency, central tendency, dispersion
Analysis using inferential statistics	Calculate: Correlation, regression,
	Test hypothesis: Chi-square, T-test, ANOVA

Qualitative data analysis

Once the transcriptions are complete, researchers should review all the data. This review should be conducted with an open mind rather than a preconceived idea of the results. At this stage of the analysis, researchers must let the data reveal insights rather than impose ideas that were formed while conducting the research. While the impressions formed during the research are important and should be retained, it is also important for researchers to look at the data with fresh eyes. It might be that comments and ideas which were initially overlooked can now be seen as being important. When reporting research results, it is these types of comments that can provide a narrative and give meaning to the recommendations (Samuels 2020).

Coding comments

Once data have been transcribed and reviewed, researchers will begin to code recurring themes. Coding is used to note the repetition of ideas, opinions, or facts. The first coding will be conducted to examine the data for answers to the research question. For example, the research question might have asked how a visit to the dentist could be made more pleasant. A focus group of clients would be asked for their ideas for improvements that could be made to a dental clinic. A transcript would be coded for the times when any mention of the ideas for improvements was mentioned. These instances are coded so that researchers can then return to the information to analyse if many of the responses gave similar ideas or if any unique suggestions were provided. This process can now be automated using technology (Yanhs 2018). Both written transcripts and videos can be analysed by software to find these recurring themes. This approach reduces the longer period of time it has traditionally taken to perform qualitative analysis. It also saves money by reducing the need for professional analysis.

Categories

Once researchers have finished coding for concepts, they may find that some need to be further broken down into categories. These concepts and categories are important as they are the building blocks from which researchers will make their recommendations for action. For example, many comments in a transcript may involve the concept of the price of a product. Several participants may state that they don't buy a product unless it is on sale. Other participants may state that they buy a competing product because it is cheaper, while some may state directly that the price of a product is too high. While all of these involve the price of a product, a researcher may decide they are too dissimilar and break them down into three categories: 'don't buy because can't afford', 'competing product purchasers', and 'non-purchasers'. The researcher may then make different recommendations for attracting each of the first two groups and recommend no action on the third.

Using coding to develop recommendations

Once coding is completed, all material will be reviewed again to develop recommendations based on the coded concepts and categories. For example, a research question might have asked, 'Why do consumers not purchase automobiles produced by our company?' The coded material may have revealed infrequent comments made on colour, appearance, and amount of chrome. All of these comments the researcher will code under one concept – 'style'. Other comments made about the cost of the automobile, a researcher will code under the concept of 'price'. Further analysis might now reveal that the concept of 'price' is two categories, not one. The first involves comments on the cost of the automobile. A separate category is now needed for those comments that involve the cost of maintaining such an automobile, including comments about gas mileage, insurance, and repair costs. Based on this coding, researchers might recommend that promotional material should address the reasonable cost of maintaining the vehicle and not just the low purchase price.

Software tools for coding

Software tools that assist in the analysis of qualitative data are now available. However, marketing researchers must decide if it is worth the money to purchase such software. If a research process has only involved one or two focus groups or interviews, the time saved in using software may not justify its cost and the time it will take for researchers to learn to use it. In this case, researchers may decide to rely on hand coding and analysis.

Analysis of observational and ethnography research data

The information provided by observational research will not be in a verbal format. Instead, the data will be in the form of notes on behaviour, photos, or video. Observation forms and notes must also be analysed, but not by coding for words. Instead, researchers will be looking for unique or repeated behaviour that has been noted on the forms or in the photos or videos. Researchers can look for these data concerning the process of using a product, new ways of using a product, where consumers use a product, and the mistakes they make when using a product – all of which may have been noted on the forms.

For example, observational research of consumers shopping at a clothing store can show how they travel through the store, which products they tend to buy first, and how long they spend in the store. If researchers notice that people seem to have a problem finding the fitting rooms, better signage may be recommended. In addition, if it becomes obvious that certain clothing racks are not being visited, it might be recommended that the store layout be changed. All of this information can then be used by management to make the store more user-friendly. The challenge when analysing the data is that it may be difficult to determine the reason for the behaviour that is observed (Poytner 2020). For example, the signage may have been ignored because the shoppers were not fluent in the language. The short period of time spent in the store may not have been in the control of the shopper because they were using their lunch break.

Often ethnography research may reveal that people use a product in a way that was not originally intended by the company that designed that product. These insights can be used to make recommendations on the redesign of a product or the development of a totally new product. For example, a study may have been conducted on students living together in university-owned housing. An analysis of discussions on sites used by students may have found that students like to study while lying on their beds. From this study, it might be recommended that better lighting be provided above beds.

Discussion questions

1   Why do researchers try to prove the null hypothesis false rather than true?
2   Why does a researcher need to know about statistical testing even if he or she doesn't understand how the math is calculated?
3   How would you describe the mode, median, and mean of the answers to a question on income level?
4   If a study finds men and women spend the same mean amount of money on clothes, what additional information would standard deviation supply?
5   Why is the analysis of qualitative data an entirely different process from the analysis of quantitative data?
6   Why is it important to organize the data from qualitative research as soon as possible after the completion of the study?
7   Why is it recommended that a researcher transcribe the tapes of a research study?

Answer these questions to continue creating a marketing research plan

1   What type of statistical analysis will be used on quantitative data?
2   How will the hypothesis be tested?

3   How will themes be found in qualitative data?
4   How will the data from observational research be analysed?

References

Dykes, Brent. "Actionable Insights: The Missing Link Between Data and Business Value." *Forbes.* April 26, 2016. www.forbes.com/sites/brentdykes/2016/04/26/actionable-insights-the-missing-link-between-data-and-business-value/?sh=2a1afe9e51e5. Accessed April 10, 2021.

Hermann, Jaryd. "Five Steps to Faster Market Research." *Forbes.* November 23, 2020. www.forbes.com/sites/theyec/2020/11/23/five-steps-to-faster-market-research/?sh=5a191279890f. Accessed March 21, 2021.

Madsbjerg, Christian and Mikkel B. Rasmussen. "The Power of 'Thick' Data." *Wall Street Journal.* March 21, 2014. www.wsj.com/articles/SB10001424052702304256404579449254114659882. Accessed April 14, 2021.

Poytner, Ray. "Observational Data has Problems: Are Researchers Aware of Them?" *GreenBook.* October 15, 2020. www.greenbook.org/mr/market-research-methodology/researchers-should-be-aware-of-the-problems-with-observational-data/. Accessed April 24, 2021.

Samuels, Rachel. "From Reporting to Analysis: How Storytelling with Data Helps Secure Executive Buy-in." *Sprout Social.* March 2, 2020. https://sproutsocial.com/insights/storytelling-with-data/. Accessed March 4, 2021.

Yanhs, Ken. "How to Love Qualitative Data at the Speed and Price of Quantitative Analysis." *Forbes.* October 26, 2018. www.forbes.com/sites/forbescommunicationscouncil/2018/10/26/how-to-love-qual-data-at-the-speed-and-price-of-quant-data/?sh=4574b14723b9. Accessed April 2, 2021.

9 Preparing reports

Importance of the written report

Marketing researchers do not conduct research just for the sake of 'knowing'. Research is conducted to find a solution to a problem. Even though the data have been collected and analysed, marketing researchers' work is still not done. After all, the analysis that the marketing researchers have completed does not solve management's problem. Instead, it is the raw material that provides the insights that researchers will use to make the recommendations that will solve the problem. Once researchers have completed the analysis and developed the recommendations, the next step is to communicate this information in a written and oral format that is both understandable and actionable.

Reasons for preparing a report

Unfortunately, too often researchers do not allocate enough time or importance to report preparation which is the last step in the research process. Perhaps this is because researchers enjoy conducting the research more than report preparation and writing. As a result, researchers might simply prefer to move on to the next research project.

However, there are important reasons why a written report is necessary. First, the report gives legitimacy to any recommendations by describing the research methodology. There is also a need to preserve information for the future. A report also communicates recommendations while providing documentation that can be used to clarify any misunderstandings. After all, the company that commissioned the research will be paying for recommendations that can be implemented to improve their performance, rather than just facts based on findings. One of the advantages of using an outside marketing research agency to conduct the study is that it can bring a fresh perspective (Powell 2020). Because no staff in the organization commissioning

DOI: 10.4324/9781003165194-10

the work has been involved in conducting the research, the report will be the only source of information.

Today there are other methods used to present research findings than a traditional written report. For example, reports can be prepared in the form of videos. This type of report is more common when conducting research with trendy products and young research participants. A video can capture 'attitudes' that are difficult to communicate in writing. Even reports that are written can benefit from video clips that show either parts of the research project or the actions of consumers. Such clips can help emotionally engage the audience.

Researchers must prepare a thorough report as management may not be able to understand the research methodology or the analysis process without a clear explanation. Terms such as 'stratified sample', 'projective techniques', and 'confidence level' may have no meaning to those whose responsibility it is to make decisions based on the research. Without an explanation of these terms, the data will either be meaningless or misunderstood. A second reason for a written report is so that the knowledge that is obtained from the research continues to be available in the future. The research data and recommendations need to be maintained for both the marketing department and management. All companies have personnel changes, and it is particularly common for marketing professionals to change positions frequently. An important purpose of the report is not only to report data or information. The written report is where the recommendations that result from the data and analysis are explained. A final reason for writing the report is to ensure that the marketing researchers who have conducted the research have a document that details findings and conclusions in case of future misunderstanding.

Marketing research ethics

Ethics provide guidelines when an individual needs to determine what actions are right and good and which are not. Ethics used in daily life are learned from families and other places such as religious organizations and schools. These learned ethical principles can be used as guidelines on how to act in interpersonal relationships. Organizations also have ethical principles that guide the relationships between the employees of the organization, its customers, and the community in which it exists. A code of conduct, a formal statement by an organization of which actions are allowed and which are prohibited, is based on ethics.

Ethical standards are important in marketing research to protect the integrity of the field and to protect participants, especially children, from harm. Social media presents unique ethical issues because of the difficulty of determining the age of respondents and the need to protect the privacy of the participants. It needs to be remembered that all marketing research depends on input from consumers. The information that is gathered does not belong only to the researchers (MacDonald 2018). The facts and opinions provided are simply borrowed and need to be treated with respect. They should not be sold or shared without informing the research participant of the purpose.

Types of research report

One size does not fit all when preparing research reports. More than one type of report may be needed. First, preliminary reports may be prepared to reassure those who commissioned the research that any efforts are on track. In addition, different groups of individuals will have a desire and need for varying levels of detail in the report. These groups include the marketing staff, management, company employees, and participants. When preparing the various reports required, researchers should consider carefully both the length of the report and how it is to be disseminated.

If the research process spans a considerable length of time, a marketing researcher may prepare a brief preliminary report. A preliminary report can assure management that the research is proceeding as planned. Having read the report, those who originally commissioned the research may decide to make changes in the methodology based on the preliminary results that have been presented. It is better to find that management wants changes before the process is complete. Of course, a more detailed report will be prepared after the research and analysis have been finished.

A report being prepared for the marketing staff of an organization should contain all details of planning and methodology. Marketing researchers will be interested in all of the results and analysis, whereas management will only be interested in the main findings. This document will also be used for reference when planning future research.

A report prepared for the management of an organization will provide an overview of the research process. Management will generally not have the time or inclination to involve themselves in all the details of the process. However, they will usually want more information on any findings and recommendations. A shorter report that leaves out most of the technical details has the advantage of being less expensive both to write and reproduce. In addition, researchers should remember that a shorter report is more likely to be read and understood. Because managers are busy with many responsibilities, a long report may be put aside to be read 'later' when there is more time. Unfortunately, this 'later' with ample free time for reading the report may never arrive. Researchers working together with management from the beginning of the research process will prove advantageous for both.

The reporting can be continued even after the research has been conducted and the report released. The recommendations based on the report may have been enthusiastically endorsed. However this does not mean that the implementation of the recommendations actually improved the performance of the company. The people responsible for the recommendations should follow up with a report on the change in key performance indicators (Finkel 2021). For example, if the recommendations were to improve sales, periodic reports should be issued on sales performance.

Components of a written report

Reports may vary in writing style, but all reports should contain an introduction, a section on methodology, any findings and recommendations, and appendices. The introduction will identify those involved in the research and provide a brief overview of the contents. The next section of the report will explain the research question, objectives, and methodology. The third section would discuss the research findings and recommendations. The appendices will provide background information that will more fully explain the report's contents.

Introduction

The introductory material contained in a report will include a title page, a letter of transmittal, a table of contents and an executive summary. The report will start with a title page that provides the name of the research study, the date of the report submittal, the names of the researchers, the names of the people or organization that commissioned the research and contact information for both groups. A letter or memo of transmittal will be included for marketing research studies that were conducted by an outside firm. The letter of transmittal formally concludes the research study and transmits ownership of the information contained in the report to the management of the company. The letter will also describe the legal ownership of any supporting material, such as tapes or completed survey forms. Because of the sensitive nature of some research, the commissioning organization may wish to have this information destroyed and in this case the letter will also state that this has been done.

The report should next contain a table of contents and should be indexed in some way so that each section can be easily found. This table of contents and the indexing are useful when the report is discussed in meetings, as each section can be easily and quickly located. A table of contents should not only list the main sections, such as the introduction and findings, it should also list the pages for any subtopics under the main topics. A table of contents should also provide a separate listing for any graphs and tables. The more detail that is provided in a table of contents, the more easily material can be found.

An executive summary quickly states the research question, the methodology, findings, and conclusions. As most people in positions of management are under time pressure, the executive summary is essential to communicate quickly what a report contains. In addition, if the executive summary does not communicate effectively that the research methodology, findings, and recommendations are important, the report may never be read. While included early on in the report, the executive summary is actually the last part that is written.

Research methodology

The body of a report will include information on the research question, the research objectives, and the research methodology. First, the problem that resulted in the research being conducted should be explained and the main and any secondary research questions should be stated. Since the findings and recommendations should directly address the research question; it should be highlighted from the body of the report by using boldface or italics so it can be easily referred to later.

The research objectives should also be explained. If they are not included, anyone reading the report may wonder why certain aspects of the research findings are not discussed further in the recommendations. For example, a research objective might have been to discover what percentage of current customers would be interested in buying a product produced in new colours. The findings might contain information discovered during focus groups that customers are not aware of the company's promotional material. While this interesting fact might be included, it will not be expounded upon, as it was not the purpose for conducting the research.

This section of the report should also describe the sample selection process. It should clearly explain how it was determined who should participate in the study and how these specific individuals were chosen from the total population. The legitimacy of the findings of a quantitative study depends upon whether the appropriate people were asked to participate. Even for qualitative research, if the wrong people are asked to participate in the research, the information will not be relevant. Therefore, to give legitimacy to the research findings and recommendations, it is important to describe the profile of participants and how they were selected.

Finally, the body of a report will explain the research methodology. In a survey, this will include how the questionnaire was developed and tested. The report will also inform the reader of how many surveys were conducted, the method of contact, and the dates of the research. For a focus group, similar information will be included but the name of the moderator will also be given. Readers may be less familiar with research techniques such as observation, projective techniques, and ethnography. If less well-known research techniques have been used, the report will need to explain the methodology in more detail.

Findings and recommendations

The next section should discuss the research findings and recommendations. This section should include a summarization of the research findings. It should not provide all the data that were compiled during the research process; instead, it should summarize the data that were used to develop the recommendations.

Research always provides a wealth of information. However, providing all the detail at this point in the report will only confuse the reader. For example, a survey might have been conducted to discover what sports respondents enjoy playing. The research will have also asked survey respondents demographic information. During the analysis stage, researchers discovered that the geographic location of participants' homes made no difference to preference. This fact will be stated. However, there is now no need to present a detailed breakdown of the home location of each participant in the body of the report. This data can be added in the appendix. On the other hand, if age was a very important variable that affected what sports people wanted to play, detailed information on age and activity preference should be included in the body of the report.

Recommendations are the most important component of a research report. After all, researchers are not paid just to collect data. They are also paid to analyse and interpret the data. The recommendations should directly address the research question and the research objectives. The concern that research proves useful, and it doesn't just sit on someone's desk, is not new. There has been increasing attention paid to this issue, as some business owners do not know how to use research for obtaining recommendations.

Appendices

The final section of the research report will provide the full data that were obtained during the research process. These could be in the form of printed tables of data, or the data can be provided electronically. It will also include information that provides further details on the research sample and methodology. For example, details on the research sampling method can be explained. If referrals were used, the organization and individuals contacted can be listed. Examples of the research methodology such as survey forms, projective techniques, and focus group scripts can also be included.

Writing a professional report

If the research report is going to be read, instead of just sitting on someone's desk, it is important that it be readable, interesting, and concise. A report that contains too much jargon, is poorly organized, and is visually unattractive will not be read. This is especially the case because most people have multiple tasks to accomplish each day and will complete the easiest task first.

Issues that researchers should consider before writing a report must include the writing style. It is as important that a report be written in the right style as that it provides the right information. Before beginning to write a report, researchers should determine for whom the report is being prepared. If a report is being written for someone in the marketing department, a more professional style will be used. Here it can be assumed that the reader will be familiar with research terminology. However, if the report is being written for someone who runs a small business, researchers must write in a more colloquial style while being careful to explain every term.

Any report should also be interesting to read. Researchers should not just state facts but also give examples of interesting incidents that occurred during the research process. This type of detail will help to bring the information to life in the mind of the reader. Another way to add interest to a report is to use photos of the participants as they were involved in the research process. If this is not possible actual quotes can be used to give the readers a feeling that they were at the research sessions.

Table 9.1 Components of a research report

Introduction	Title page
	Letter or memo of transmittal
	Table of contents
	Executive summary
Research methodology	Introduction
	Research question
	Research objectives
	Sample selection
	Methodology
Findings and recommendations	Findings
	Recommendations
Appendices	Further details on sampling procedure
	Examples of methodology
	Full presentation of data

A report should be kept as short as possible while still including all necessary information. Because management employees are short on time, any long report or presentation will not be useful (Valentine 2020). It should also be arranged so that readers can process the amount of information they wish without necessarily reading the entire report. This can be accomplished by providing a well-written executive summary and clearly labelling each section. In addition, headings and subheadings should be used throughout the report so that a specific issue can be found quickly.

Oral presentation

An oral presentation is an opportunity for researchers both to explain and to 'sell' to management any research findings and recommendations. An oral presentation also allows researchers to provide a more effective description of the research methodology. This is because during an oral presentation, a presenter, by observing their audience, can become aware of when they are encountering difficulty in understanding and can explain any confusing details more fully. In addition, a presenter can more clearly explain how report recommendations are related to any research findings. Finally, an oral presentation provides a means to clarify any misunderstandings about the research process.

Technology makes communication across time and distance easy. When it is impossible to meet in person, then the only method for presenting an oral report may be using video technology. Most people have become comfortable with this type of communication. Research has shown that the more complex the information that is being communicated, the less effective technologically mediated means of communication become (Kumar and Epley 2020). For complex information, reading the social cues given off by non-visual expressions and tone of voice alerts the speaker to when clarification is needed.

Presentation structure

Presentations, just like written reports, must have a structure for two reasons. A structure helps the audience anticipate, and concentrate on, information that is of particular interest. A structure also helps a presenter stay on topic. No one would throw together a written report at the last minute as its poor organization would leave readers confused. It would be obvious to them that researchers had not taken time to present the material in a logical manner.

However, people do throw presentations together at the last moment and believe that their audience will not notice. Unfortunately, a poorly prepared oral presentation will leave listeners just as confused as a poorly prepared written report. A well-prepared presentation will have four major components: an introduction, methodology, findings and recommendations, and a conclusion. It is important when planning a presentation that most time is devoted to the recommendations section. Before the presentation the time needed for each section should be noted to ensure that all topics will be covered before the conclusion of the presentation. Not all sections need to be given equal time as not all have equal importance.

The attention span of people has dramatically shrunk because of the speed of electronic communication (Patel 2019). People have become accustomed to messages that are short and concise. One idea for grabbing the attention of the audience is to start with the report's recommendations as this provides an incentive to listen to the presentation. The attention span of the listeners will depend on the type of audience. However, it is always better to under- than overestimate and keep the presentation as short as possible.

The presentation's introduction should identify the researchers and the commissioning company. It also should explain how long the presentation will take. During the introduction, the presenter should inform the audience whether questions may be asked during the presentation or if the audience should keep their questions until the end. The introduction should then very quickly state the research question and describe what information the presentation will contain.

The section of the presentation on methodology is where the presenter will first state the research question and objectives. The presenter will then briefly inform the audience of how the research participants were selected. The presentation should not be used to describe the technical details of the sampling procedure. If the audience is interested, the report will contain all the necessary information. The purpose of describing the sampling procedure during the presentation is simply to give credibility to the findings and recommendations. The same holds true for the methodology, although more time should be spent on this topic so the audience will better understand how the findings were obtained. At this point in the presentation, a sample survey form can be distributed, projective techniques can be displayed, or a short video clip from a focus group can be shown.

The presenter should spend more time presenting the findings and recommendations. They can use visuals such as graphs to quickly show to the audience what has been learned from the research. The presentation should never try to explain all the findings, as there simply isn't the time and the audience will get lost in the details. In addition, it is the presenter's responsibility to sift through all the findings to determine what is relevant for answering the research question. However, any findings that have an impact on the recommendations should be presented.

Table 9.2 Sample outline for presentation with time percentage

Introduction (10%)	Identify research participants
	State time allotted for presentation
	Inform when questions can be asked
	Describe contents of presentation
Methodology (20%)	Statement of research question and objectives
	Brief explanation of sample selection procedure
	Description of methodology
Recommendations: (60%)	Description of findings
	Recommendations for action
Conclusion (10%)	Restatement of research question
	Review of main recommendations
	Thank audience and ask for questions

The conclusion to a presentation should be brief. The presenter should restate the research questions and the main recommendations. They should also thank the audience for their attention. The presenter should allow adequate time to answer any questions. The audience should also be informed of who it is they can contact if they have any questions in the future.

Presentation rules

A presentation has a different purpose than that of a written report. Giving a good presentation is a skill that can be learned. Everyone understands that being able to produce a clear, concise, and interesting written report takes time and effort. However, too often presentations are afterthoughts that people expect will happen automatically once they are in front of an audience. After all, while not everyone is skilled in writing, everyone can speak. Yet nothing could be further from the truth.

The general rules for an effective presentation are to be interesting, organized, and brief. A presentation should never be thought of as simply an oral presentation of all the information in a written report. The purpose of a presentation is not just to communicate information. After all, the audience at a presentation can read the written report for themselves. The purpose of a presentation is to 'sell' the ideas contained in the report by persuading an audience to act upon its recommendations. If an oral presentation is successful, the audience should be eager to read the written report for more details.

Presentation problems

A successful presentation depends on preparation. In addition, a good presentation must be interesting. If it is not interesting, the research recommendations may be ignored because the audience simply lost their attention in what they heard. Everyone has probably had the experience of having to sit through a poorly prepared presentation.

There are actions that are guaranteed to result in a poor-quality presentation. A presenter should never read anything longer than a short quotation. After all, the audience came to hear an oral presentation and they could have stayed in their offices to read the report on their own. In addition, audiences should never be frustrated by being shown any PowerPoint slides or other visuals that can't be easily read. They should also never be bored as life is difficult enough without struggling to stay awake during a presentation. A presenter should never be so rude as to ignore the audience, nor should they overwhelm an audience with too much detail. It should be remembered that humans can only assimilate so much information at a time. Finally, a presenter should demonstrate enthusiasm about the information that is being presented.

Discussion questions

1　What types of reports need to be prepared and how do they differ?
2　Why is the recommendations section the most important component of a written report?
3　Why should the writer of a report ensure that it is readable, interesting, and concise?
4　Why should quantitative information be presented using tables and charts?
5　Why should a researcher take the time to prepare an oral presentation when the audience can read the written report at a time and place of their choosing?
6　When should either low-tech or high-tech information be used when making an oral presentation?

Answer these questions to continue creating a marketing research plan

1　How will the findings and recommendations be reported?
2　What type of written reports will need to be prepared?
3　What form will the oral presentation take?

References

Finkel, David. "Streamline Your Marketing Reports with these 4 Tips." *Inc*. January 14, 2021. www.inc.com/david-finkel/streamline-your-marketing-reports-with-these-4-tips.html. Accessed March 31, 2021.

Kumar, Amit and Nicholas Epley. "Research: Type Less, Talk More." *Harvard Business Review*. October 5, 2020. https://hbr.org/2020/10/research-type-less-talk-more. Accessed April 3, 2021.

MacDonald, Scott. "A Code of Ethics in Research." *Forbes*. April 9, 2018. www.forbes.com/sites/scottmcdonald1/2018/04/09/a-code-of-ethics-in-research/?sh=618ea788cf9a. Accessed January 24, 2020.

Patel, Deep. "14 Proven Ways to Improve Your Communication Skills." *Entrepreneur*. May 15, 2019. www.entrepreneur.com/article/300466. Accessed April 22, 2021.

Powell, Terry. "Marketing Research Studies: Three Tips for Doing Them Right." *Forbes*. March 5, 2020. www.forbes.com/sites/forbescoachescouncil/2020/03/05/market-research-studies-three-tips-for-doing-them-right/?sh=3891d3ad4b16. Accessed January 13, 2021.

Valentine, Matthew. "Does Marketing Research Need to 'Loosen Up'?". *Marketing Week*. December 1, 2020. www.marketingweek.com/market-research-fix-image-problem/. Accessed February 25, 2021.

Index

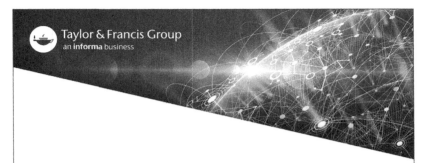

Printed in the United States
by Baker & Taylor Publisher Services